OUTSIDE

JAMIE DURIE
OUTSIDE

CREATING YOUR PERFECT OUTDOOR ROOM

JAMIE DURIE PUBLISHING

HarperCollins*Publishers*
in association with
Jamie Durie Publishing

First published in Australia in 2008
by HarperCollins*Publishers* Australia Pty Limited
ABN 36 009 913 517
www.harpercollins.com.au

HarperCollins*Publishers*
25 Ryde Road, Pymble, Sydney, NSW 2073, Australia
31 View Road, Glenfield, Auckland 10, New Zealand
1–A, Hamilton House, Connaught Place, New Delhi – 110 001, India
77–85 Fulham Palace Road, London W6 8JB, United Kingdom
2 Bloor Street East, 20th floor, Toronto, Ontario M4W 1A8, Canada
10 East 53rd Street, New York NY 10022, USA

Jamie Durie Publishing
JPD Media Pty Ltd
ABN 83 098 894 761
35 Albany Street, Crows Nest, NSW 2065, Australia

FOUNDER AND EDITORIAL DIRECTOR: Jamie Durie
GROUP CREATIVE DIRECTOR: Nadine Bush

PUBLISHER: Nicola Hartley
DEVELOPMENTAL EDITOR: Bettina Hodgson
GARDEN DESIGN: Jamie Durie
STYLING: Nadine Bush
TEXT DEVELOPMENT: Nicola Hartley and Bettina Hodgson
TECHNICAL CONSULTANTS: Giselle Barron, Sebastian Tesoriero, Michael Wild, Georgina Reid
EDITOR: Stephanie Goodwin
CONCEPT DESIGN: Amanda Emmerson
DESIGNER: Avril Makula
INTERNATIONAL PHOTOGRAPHY: Jamie Durie
GARDEN PHOTOGRAPHY: Jason Busch
GARDEN CONSTRUCTION: Landart Landscapes

National Library of Australia Cataloguing-in-Publication data

Author: Durie, Jamie.
Title: Outside / Jamie Durie.
ISBN: 978 0 7322 8861 7 (hbk.)
Subjects: Gardens--Design. Landscape gardening. Landscape design.
Other Authors/Contributors:
Durie, Jamie. Outside.
Dewey Number: 712.6

Cover design by Natalie Winter
Cover photography by Jason Busch
Set in Gotham on InDesign
Printed and bound in China by Toppan Printing Co on 157gsm Chinese Matt Art

5 4 3 2 1   08 09 10 11

contents

What makes a garden an extension of our home—a private sanctuary in which to relax and reflect upon our day, and break bread with family and friends? Is it a question of function, of comfort, of creating a space that represents our lifestyle, design choices and own personal tastes, or is it simply just about being outdoors—catching the breeze, watching the sun set, listening to the evening quiet—and letting nature soothe our souls? I believe it is all these things. That it is about taking the inside out and the outside in to create a space that inspires; that makes you want to be there. I call this place the outdoor room.

The Outdoor Room—my new TV show, which this book is based on—is a celebration of these ideas and one that the team and I are very proud of. It is the show I've been waiting to make for ten years—a combination of everything I've learned from the great producers, cameramen, editors, photographers and cast I've been surrounded by for the last few years. And of course then there is the inspiration I get from you guys at home, as well as from the hundreds of families we've built gardens for and what they've taught me about themselves, their families and their needs for their own private gardens. It is also the result of over 20 years of travel and designing gardens in many different countries, and the desire to share what I've learned with as many people as possible.

Throughout the years I have developed an immense appreciation for the lessons learned from international travel—from the people and traditions of individual cultures, including design and building methods, lifestyle responses to climate and culture, natural and innovative materials, and plants and planting schemes that are native to or characteristic of specific regions. The essence of *The Outdoor Room* is to visit these countries—explore their architectural, cultural and design traditions—then take the best of these ideas and adapt them to the Australian lifestyle, climate, and of course to the families we're creating gardens for. By reading this book, you're now a part of the very first series of the show and all my years of dreaming.

The Outdoor Room concept is particularly relevant to Australia, because—being a multicultural country with little more than 200 years since European settlement and great diversity in climate and topography—we are open to international ideas and not so inhibited by old traditions. Instead, we are interested in forging our own identity and as such are at the forefront of Eurasian-fusion-style landscape design, which is evident in the gardens I've created for the show.

In making the show, my aim was not to go to a country with a shopping list of pre-empted ideas, but to go there and immerse myself in the culture—to come away with raw, authentic experiences. We went to centuries-old palaces and dined on the floor with locals in India; we visited pottery studios in Italy and markets and textile factories in Mexico; we carved wood sculptures and discovered the importance of silk worms in Thailand; visited game parks and sang with choirs in South Africa and meditated in tatami rooms in Japan. Most importantly, we were able to leave some of these experiences with the owners of the gardens I created from my personal experience.

This book follows the same format as the TV series, but offers a closer look at the finished gardens as well as additional information and practical tips on how you can adapt these ideas to your own outdoor space. The beauty of this show is that the gardens featured in this book were designed and constructed on a budget and built within a matter of days, so there are hundreds of achievable ideas behind the designs that can be adapted to any size space—whether you are building from scratch or simply updating an existing space. So go for it ... these ideas are yours for the taking.

Enjoy!

a japanese dining room

a land of striking natural beauty and artistic sensibility, the worship of nature and art is intrinsic to Japanese culture, design and tradition.

Situated in northeastern Asia, Japan's diverse topography and climate produces four true seasons. From the cherry blossoms of spring to the burnished tones of autumn, each season is revered for the natural change of foliage and the ritual celebrations it brings.

Composed of four main islands, Japan is one of the most geologically active areas in the world, with around 60 active volcanoes. Its most famous volcano, the now dormant Mount Fuji, is also the country's highest peak. As mountains and natural rock formations are worshipped, most of Japan's 127 million people reside in densely populated urban areas, leaving almost 70 per cent of the country covered by forest. Sharp mountain ranges rise from the coastal plains and fast-flowing rivers run to the sea. Groves of giant moso bamboo (*Phyllostachys edulis*) thrive from the tropical south to the cool temperate north, while the interior mountains are studded with trees of birch (*Betula*), cedar (*Cedrus*), cypress (*Cupressus*) and maple (*Acer*), and azaleas (*Rhodendron*) growing wildly.

Japanese gardens are designed to depict the way these natural elements of rock, water and plants appear in nature, blending with the architecture they surround to create a single scene. Like a landscape painting, the balanced composition of these micro naturescapes are intended to be viewed and meditated upon from vantage points within the home, temple or tea house, or strolled through as if passing through a landscape.

Unique to Japan, the spatial art of Japanese landscape gardening dates back to the Asuka Period (592–710) and has its roots in Buddhist religion. Expressions of patience and harmonious simplicity, Japanese gardens fall into three main styles: *tsukiyama*, *karesansui* and *chaniwa*. A *tsukiyama* garden is arranged to show nature in miniature, with hills, waterfalls, arched bridges and ponds. A *karesansui* garden, influenced by Zen Buddhism, is a more abstract reproduction of a natural landscape and features the arrangement of sand and gravel, representative of rivers and the sea, around symbolically placed rocks. The *chaniwa* is the garden adjacent to a ceremonial tea house, and includes such elements as stone basins with ladles (*tsukubai*) to wash hands and mouths before entering the tea house, stone lanterns (*ishidoro*), stepping stones (*tobi-ishi*) and natural planting.

Plants, including bonsai, are limited in the Japanese garden, and like other symbolic elements, each has a reason for its placement. A meditative art form, tending gardens in Japan is approached as if worshipping at a temple, much like the Japanese arts of ikebana, calligraphy and origami.

The Japanese people, concerned as they are with beauty, simplicity and form, are also master craftsmen. They produce products such as tatami mats, carved stone sculptures and lanterns, and Japanese silk and rice paper, which is used for everything from notepaper to building materials.

inspired design ideas

MINIATURISING NATURE

Japanese gardens represent a large landscape on a small scale. Copying nature in a balanced composition, their design implies a sense of serenity and unspoiled beauty.

SUNKEN DINING

Traditional Japanese *horikotatsu* dining and seating features a customary small table—approximately the height of a Western coffee table—with a sunken area beneath for feet and a cushion upon which to sit.

JAPANESE MAPLE

Japanese maples (*Acer palmatum* Dissectum group cv) are popular in Japan for their blazing autumn foliage and form. Native to Japan, China and North Korea, there are over 400 varieties of Japanese maple. They also make excellent bonsai subjects.

TRADITIONAL JAPANESE ORNAMENTS

Traditional ornaments such as stone lanterns (*ishidoro*) and basins (*tsukubai*) are popular inclusions in the Japanese garden. Paper screens (*shoji*) and lanterns (*chochin*) are popular interior inclusions that work equally well in an outdoor room.

japan at home

This large, overgrown garden had little in the way of outdoor living space or level areas in which to create them. What it did have was an abundance of natural rock and a stunning bushland setting.

Taking inspiration from the natural environment—in particular natural stone—and incorporating these elements into the design is an integral part of Japanese architectural philosophy; the first rule being that the design must suit the site, not the other way around. I thought this was a perfect starting point in envisaging a design for this site.

The first thing I wanted to create was a functional space for the owners to relax and entertain in. Drawing upon the Japanese influence, I created two main spaces—a cooking and dining area and a living room in which to retreat and enjoy the garden view.

Each space features traditional Japanese elements. The living room was laid with tatami mats cut around existing sandstone boulders, while the rear walls were created from Perspex inlaid with grasses and then backlit to give the appearance of *shoji* screens. Traditional Kyoto-style sliding restaurant doors—80 years old and made from cedar—were installed in the front and side of the tatami room, adding a sense of authenticity and intrigue to the design.

The dining room, linked to the living room by a deck of warm timber, features a granite-topped table with integrated *teppanyaki* grill, sunken into the deck and inspired by just about every restaurant I have ever been to in Japan. The aim of the built-in design was to allow more visual space by not cluttering the deck with outdoor furniture and to give the owners the feeling of being embraced by the garden.

Behind the dining table, we turned the existing sandstone wall into a dramatic feature by cantilevering sandstone shelves to create platforms for a bonsai display. With a stone lantern behind and paper lanterns above, the wall is a stunning feature day or night. A country-style Japanese pot of Timor black bamboo (*Bambusa lako*) and a Japanese maple (*Acer palmatum* Dissectum group cv) growing out of a circular cut in the deck completes the traditional look.

The Japanese garden is all about miniaturising nature, and the inclusion of bonsais and a dry river bed of crushed quartz and large quartz boulders built into the deck—symbolic of a fresh flowing stream—were my tributes to this philosophy.

Surrounding the living and dining areas, the natural bushland was regenerated by a visit from the local council and Landcare group, who pulled out all the weeds and other introduced species and replaced them with native species. This was integrated with the Japanese concept by planting a wall of shining burrawang (*Lepidozamia peroffskyana*), flax lilies (*Dianella caerulea*), bird's nest ferns (*Asplenium australasicum*), Gymea lilies (*Doryanthes excelsa*) and native violets (*Viola banksii*).

The overall result is an outdoor room that is a living, breathing integration of indoor and outdoor living.

1

SCALE 1:50

MARBLO PANEL WINDOW

ADDITIONAL PLANTING TO COMPL
15 x *Asplenium australasicum*
10 x *Doryanthes excelsa*
30 x *Viola banksii*

SELECTED BONSAI

SUNKEN HARDWOOD TIMBER TABL

CANTILEVERED SANDSTONE OR TI
DISPLAY SHELVES

10 x *Platycerium bifurcatum* ALONG

TIMBER DECK OVER EXISTING PAVING—
REFER TO DETAIL

TATAMI MATS OVER MARINE PLY FLOOR

SLATE ROOF TO TATAMI ROOM
3000 x 3000MM

EXCAVATE OUT EXISTING BBQ
ROCK

ADDITIONAL PLANTING TO COMPLEMENT
EXISTING

SHOJI SLIDING DOORS TO EITHER
SIDE OF PAVILION

400 x 400 RECYCLED TIMBER POSTS
WITH LINTEL TO FORM STRUCTURE
FOR TATAMI ROOM

3 x NATURAL SANDSTONE
ROCK ARRANGEMENT

Acer palmatum
Dissectum *group* IN POT

GRANITE WATERBOWL AND
BAMBOO LADLE

ELECTROLUX BBQ

IRON BAR
70, 140, 7

TATAMI M

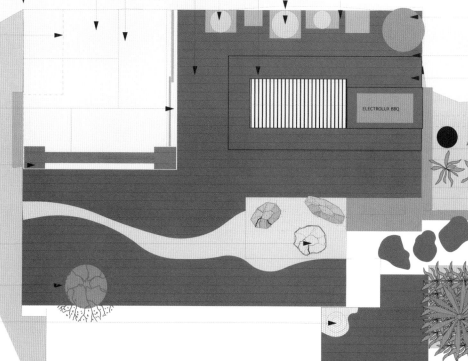

Note: Plans may vary from design to construction

CE

3 x BLACK TERRAZZO FEATURE POTS
1 x *Rhapis excelsa*

SUNKEN TIMBER PLATFORM

INTEGRATED BBQ FROM ELECTROLUX
IN BLACK GRANITE BENCHTOP

1 x *Bambusa lako*

5 x *Lepidozamia peroffskyana*
PLANTED UNDER EXISTING PALMS

20 x *Viola banksii*

5 x *Lepidozamia peroffskyana*

6 x *Pogonatherum paniceum*

NEW RETAINING WALL TO BE
CLAD IN SANDSTONE

BLACK GRANITE STEPPERS IN
WHITE GRAVEL

50 x *Dianella caerulea*

5 x *Doryanthes palmeri*

1900

DECKING
.ETC

Clockwise from left:

- Taking inspiration from Japanese *karesansui*-style rock and gravel gardens, we created a dry riverbed by cutting into the timber deck and lining it with white crushed quartz pebbles symbolising a fresh-flowing mountain stream and larger quartz boulders symbolising the mountains themselves.

- The pavilion, or *tatami* room, is built into the natural rock face of the garden and remains exposed on one side. It is made from a mixture of timber and antique Japanese sliding restaurant doors and the floor is lined with *tatami* mats sourced from Japan. A sandstone boulder jutting out from the rock wall forms a natural bench seat in the far corner of the room, while a timber log feature helps to connect the structure to the natural surrounds.

- The sandstone-clad retaining walls make a stunning textural feature in the garden. Wherever possible, all–natural materials have been incorporated into the design to blend with the bush setting—blurring the boundaries between the natural and built landscape.

Facing page:

- Sandstone shelving is built into the natural rock wall above the dining area to create a garden gallery of Japanese bonsais, and to introduce a vertical element to the design.

Facing page:

- Sandstone planter walls were installed as a feature to the entry of the garden, forming a geometric pattern that criss-crosses the landscape. The pathway is made of stone steppers and crushed quartz gravel.

This page—from top:

- A native planting theme was used throughout the garden with the additional inclusion of plants traditionally associated with Japan, including bamboo (*Bambusa lako* and *Pogonatherum paniceum*), bonsais (*Juniperus conferta*, *Liquidambar styraciflua* and *Rhodendron* Kurume) and Japanese maple (*Acer palmatum*). An existing tree provides a lovely natural canopy over the dining area and looks stunning when lit up at night by the traditional Japanese celebration lanterns hanging from its branches.

- The authentic Japanese-style sunken dining area features a stunning built-in black granite tabletop with integrated *teppanyaki* grill. Being built in, the dining area maximises deck space and minimises clutter by not needing to place additional furniture on the deck space.

design key

Create your own Japanese-style outdoor living space by incorporating some of the ideas we came up with for our garden. Taking inspiration from the natural environment and choosing design elements that suit your site, not the other way around, are good places to start.

PLANTS

TREES
- *Acer palmatum* Dissectum group cv CUTLEAF JAPANESE MAPLE (4)

BONSAIS
- *Juniperus conferta* SHORE JUNIPER
- *Liquidambar styraciflua* LIQUIDAMBAR
- *Rhodendron* Kurume hybrid AZALEA (2)

SHRUBS
- *Asplenium australasicum* BIRD'S NEST FERN
- *Bambusa lako* TIMOR BLACK BAMBOO
- *Doryanthes excelsa* GYMEA LILY
- *Doryanthes palmeri* SPEAR LILY
- *Lepidozamia peroffskyana* SHINING BURRAWANG (1)
- *Platycerium bifurcatum* ELKHORN FERN
- *Pogonatherum paniceum* MALAY PYGMY BAMBOO
- *Rhapis excelsa* LADY PALM

GROUNDCOVERS
- *Dianella caerulea* BLUE FLAX LILY
- *Viola banksii* NATIVE VIOLET

MATERIALS

WALLS
- Timber frame pavilion with traditional Japanese cedar and bamboo sliding doors (6) and rear wall of Marblo inlaid with grasses (3).
- Garden retaining walls clad in sandstone (4).

FLOORS
- Traditional Japanese tatami mats line the pavilion floor (2).
- Timber deck with cut-out dry river bed feature, lined with crushed white quartz pebbles and boulders to symolise a fresh-flowing stream (5).
- Path of stone steppers surrounded by crushed white quartz pebbles lead from the garden to the deck (1).

OVERHEAD
- Slate shingles clad the external surface of the pavilion roof.

FEATURES
- Sandstone boulders and feature shelves.
- Built-in granite-topped table with integrated Japanese *teppanyaki* grill.
- Granite water bowl and antique stone pots for the deck area.

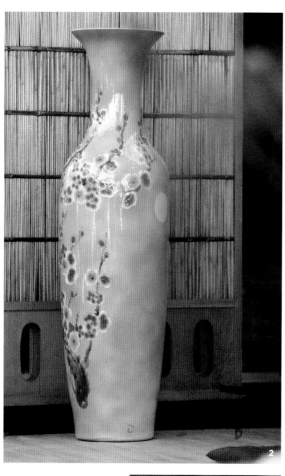

FURNITURE
AND ACCESSORIES

1 The natural, even tones of the materials palette provide the perfect background to accessorise the garden with decorative elements of vibrant colour and pattern. These Japanese paper and bamboo fans feature traditional geisha prints, and add a colourful and practical touch to the table setting.

2 This oversize vase, featuring a Japanese-style cherry blossom design, is placed on the deck in front of the sliding screens for interest and appeal.

3 Japanese lacquer-ware bowls, saki bottles and chopsticks sit atop the built-in granite-topped table. Cushions in traditional red complement the setting and provide comfort for seating.

4 Authentic Japanese celebration lanterns hang from the tree above the dining table, providing light as well as a festive atmosphere.

5 A setting made from sushi-roll mats and lacquerware is placed in the pavilion for the owner's cat.

6 Collapsible boxes made from kimono fabric keep the sake bottles warm and provide an interesting centrepiece for the table.

7 An ikebana arrangement and umbrella of silk and bamboo decorate the pavilion in typical Zen minimalist fashion.

JAMIE BROUGHT HOME:

▪ Tatami garden mats

Look out for similar Japanese and Japanese-inspired items at markets and stores in your area.

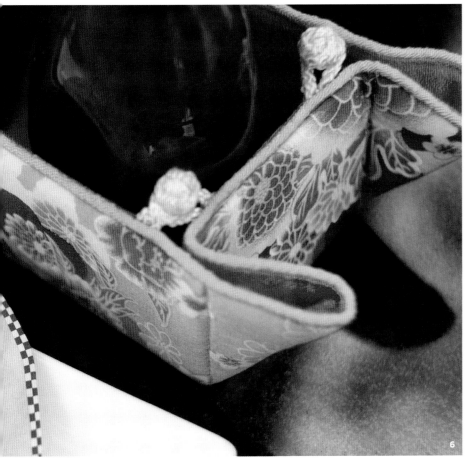

an egyptian oasis

One of the oldest civilisations, Egypt is blessed with centuries of colourful history, rich culture and old-world charm. With desert accounting for over 95 per cent of Egypt's landmass, only the Nile Valley and its surrounds are fertile, creating a raw and dramatic landscape. And yet, surprisingly, Egypt is also home to some of the oldest gardens in the world.

Perhaps due to the harsh climate, arid land and many unsettled periods in their evolution, the Egyptians recognised long ago the relief that could be found in a tranquil, shaded garden. Retreating to a cooling outdoor space was not only necessary for survival, but to balance the dramatic landscape that surrounded them. Their gardens became their own private oases, a sanctuary to shield them from the unforgiving desert, in which to cultivate food and access the healing powers of nature.

Egypt's livelihood centres around the River Nile. The abundance of running water in the Nile and its lush surrounds is in stark contrast to the burning desert that exists on either side of it and it's this distinction that has helped shape Egypt's history since time immemorial. For shipping, trade, the farming of produce and the harvesting of water, the Nile has always been, and continues to be, a critical element in the survival of the country. But more than this, the importance of the Nile and its lifeblood of water have had a massive influence on Egyptian architecture and landscaping techniques and a water theme is often found in Egyptian gardens.

Just as the Nile lies at the core of the country, sustaining the people and giving life, a pool of water or section of running water via a series of channels was historically central to many gardens, offering a tranquil environment at home and cooling the air.

Shade was also an important element, often created with wooden columns, arbours, vines and many fruit trees, which offered a source of food as well as relief from the sun. Open areas or courtyards were usually on the northern side of the home to allow for shade. Flowers were also abundant and used for colour, fragrance and decoration both inside and outside the home.

Throughout history, the Egyptians have been known for their sense of balance, order and harmony. Their architectural style, symmetrical and orderly, is reflected in the neat rows of fruit trees lining the canals, the straight edges of the great pyramids, or the high walls that often surrounded the houses or cities.

As a civilisation, they were ahead of their time in many aspects. Interestingly, even though we are obviously less reliant on the 'survival' function that an ancient garden might have offered, the design elements that were important back then are surprisingly close to those we would use in an Egyptian-inspired garden today.

inspired design ideas

WATER CHANNELS

Water was important in Egypt—not just for the cultivation of food and produce, but to cool the air. Man-made channels were built to direct the water through the cities. The wealthy often had pools of water in their courtyards.

BRASS

Egyptians have a long history of working with brass. An alloy of copper and zinc, it was the most common metal for everyday use in ancient Egypt. Today, the production of brass and copperware is still thriving and decorative pots, plates, candlesticks and lamps can create the perfect addition to an Egyptian-inspired outdoor room.

MOULDED MONUMENTS

Egypt is renowned for its straight-edged, mysterious pyramids. It is believed now that some of the stones used to build the pyramids were man-made, created by limestone poured into moulds.

POTTERY

A functional element in ancient Egypt to help carry water, store food and produce or display colourful flowers, Egyptian pottery was also ornamental and decorative. Turned upside down with a candle placed in the centre, a pot can also be used for lighting.

OASIS LIVING

For many Egyptians, their gardens formed their own private oases. Living shade formed by overhead vines, arbours, rows of fruit trees and palms, combined with ponds of water to cool the air and irrigate the plants, created relief from the harsh desert landscape and unrelenting sun.

egypt at home

Believe it or not, this Egyptian-inspired garden started out as a bare and colourless empty space. The only plant life that existed were two Bangalow palms (*Archontophoenix cunninghamiana*) in the centre of the garden. The owners had been considering removing this tree, but we've made it a central focus—just as it would have been in an authentic Egyptian oasis hundreds of years ago!

When I met with the owners, the first thing I noticed was a steel camel wind chime hanging on the back porch. They talked about their large family, connection to Middle Eastern culture and their love of entertaining—with often up to 30 family members and friends in their backyard. I immediately visualised an informal outdoor 'oasis' with a Mediterranean theme, bursting with colour, flowers and plants. They needed some paved areas for entertaining and dining, but most importantly a space that could be used all year round, to sit in and relax.

Reflective of the great pyramids, we built a tiered pergola, using metal grill, Natureed and timber to create a lattice effect and chunky columns that step up in a triangular fashion to the roof. Internally lit, the columns create a warm, evocative glow at night. Natureed was added inside each column for effect, and seating made from big chunks of sandstone helped create a rustic, authentic look.

Palms are prevalent throughout Egyptian history. We complemented the existing Bangalow palms (*Archontophoenix cunninghamiana*) with the addition of several other varieties of palms. Alexandra palms (*Archontophoenix alexandrae*) were planted in each corner of the room for symmetry and to frame the space. These are fast-growing plants which will eventually grow up and arch over the top of the pavilion, offering shade. The golden cane palms (*Dypsis lutescens*) are more compact and potting them gave us an opportunity to introduce some more colour and texture. Slow-growing pygmy date palms (*Phoenix roebelenii*) were planted down the side to give a luscious effect with dense foliage.

Fixed seating on both sides of the garden have built-in planter boxes containing papyrus—a plant symbolic of Egypt. To help create a natural look, we used Natureed to clad existing Colourbond fences. Red and white geraniums (*Pelargonium* x *hortorum*) were planted for colour and abundance and cast iron plant (*Aspidistra elatior*) and rhoeo (*Tradescantia spathacea*) frame the base of the existing palms to soften and add texture and colour.

Integral to the traditional Egyptian courtyard was water, so we built in a channel that allows water to flow lazily down the centre of the garden, stepping down with the pavers. With concrete pavers on either side, the overall look reflects the River Nile with its sandy desert on either side feeding into an oasis filled with shady palms and vibrant, coloured flowers.

14400

5250

220

2400MM HIGH TEA TREE BRUSH
CLADDING ALONG BOUNDARY AND TO
ENCLOSE COURTYARD

(12) 500 x 500 x 2400MM HIGH
COLUMNS AROUND BOUNDARY OF
COURTYARD RENDERED AND PAINTED
IN COLOUR AS SELECTED

6 x LARGE ROUND POTS PLANTED
WITH PALMS

EXISTING PALM TO REMAIN

AS SELECTED SEATING ALONG
BOUNDARY FENCE

WATER/FLAME RILL TO WIND AROUND
PALM AND THROUGH COURTYARD

NEW PAVING

SIX SEAT DINING SETTING

LANTERN AS SOURCED BY JAMIE
TO BE SUSPENDED BETWEEN COLUMNS
ABOVE DINING AREA

REMOVE EXISTING STUMP

900

4500

HERB GARDEN IN PLANTER TROUGH

BBQ AS SELECTED FROM EVEDURE
RANGE

1600MM HIGH RENDERED
WALL. COLOUR AS SELECTED

ROW OF PALMS PLANTED
IN FRONT OF WALLS TO
COURTYARD

LAWN

EXISTING
LAWN

Note: Plans may vary from design to construction

an egyptian oasis **29**

Clockwise from left:

- Two existing Bangalow palms (*Archontophoenix cunninghamiana*) were retained in the garden, forming the base of the oasis-style theme. To this we added four Alexandra palms (*Archontophoenix alexandrae*)—one on each corner of the pavilion—and potted golden cane palms (*Dypsis lutescens*) at the back of the garden. Pygmy date palms (*Phoenix roebelenii*) were then planted on either side of the lawn close to the house. Mostly hardy by nature, palms need little water once established.

- We mass planted rhoeo (*Tradescantia spathacea*) to add colour, ground cover texture and to fit in with the overall oasis theme of the garden. Prolific by nature, this plant spreads quickly to form dense coverage which reduces the amount of garden maintenance required. Pink tinges to the underside of the leaves add rich tones and visual interest.

- Hard-wearing concrete pavers in natural sandstone shades gently step down the slope of the site. The symmetrical lines of the paving and garden space are reminiscent of the geometric and ordered approach to Egyptian architecture and garden design.

- A handmade water rill running through the centre of the garden steps down over four different levels, circulating water from a reservoir at the bottom of the garden back to the top. The sound of flowing water creates a peaceful, lush atmosphere and has a cooling effect on the space. Also, because of its narrow configuration, the volume of water pumped through the feature is comparatively small, saving water by minimising evaporation. The stepping of layers is replicated in the roof design of the pavilion, which is made out of lattice and stepped up into a pyramid-inspired structure reminiscent of traditional Egyptian architecture.

- The built-in timber seating also acts as planter boxes for papyrus (*Cyperus papyrus*)—a plant typically found in Egyptian gardens. Zonal geranium (*Pelargonium* x *hortorum*) was planted for its vibrant red flowers and lush foliage—perfect for creating an abundant oasis look. The addition of cushions, rugs, stools and a hammock complements the planting scheme and enhances the oasis feel.

design key

Create your own Egyptian-style outdoor living space by incorporating some of the ideas we came up with for our garden. Sometimes your existing planting scheme might provide clues as to where to start—for example, what type of plants do and don't grow well in your area.

PLANTS

PALM TREES
- *Archontophoenix alexandrae* ALEXANDRA PALM
- *Dypsis lutescens* GOLDEN CANE PALM (1)
- *Phoenix roebelenii* PYGMY DATE PALM

SHRUBS
- *Aspidistra elatior* CAST IRON PLANT (2)
- *Elettaria cardamomum* CARDAMOM
- *Helichrysum petiolare* 'Limelight' LIMELIGHT LICORICE PLANT
- *Pelargonium* x *hortorum* ZONAL GERANIUM

GROUNDCOVERS AND GRASSES
- *Tradescantia spathacea* RHOEO (2, 3)
- *Typha* sp. CUMBUNGI

WATER PLANTS
- *Cyperus papyrus* PAPYRUS

HERBS
- *Coriandrum sativum* CORIANDER
- *Petroselinum crispum* FLAT LEAF PARSLEY
- *Mentha suaveolens* APPLE MINT

MATERIALS

WALLS
• Brushbox fencing was used to clad the existing fences and boundary walls (2).

FLOORS
• Sandstone-coloured concrete pavers are simple, hardwearing and effective (2).

OVERHEAD
• The structure of the pergola is made from timber and features a decorative lattice effect and tiered roofline inspired by the pyramids (4).

FEATURES
• Natureed cladding was combined with metal security grill and timber to build the columns of the pergola. These are lit from within to create ambient lighting (1).
• A water rill made out of copper piping runs down the centre of the garden, stepping down over several levels.
• A mass of irregular-shaped sandstone rocks forms part of the water rill feature at the bottom of the garden (3).
• Built-in timber benches with planter boxes provide additional seating down one side of the garden (2). Sandstone benches were built in on the other side.

FURNITURE
AND ACCESSORIES

1 A large brass incense burner sourced direct from Egypt makes a stunning sculptural feature.

2 Cutting holes out of these simple terracotta pots produced lovely candle-lit lanterns.

3 Additional metal lanterns dotted around the garden create an inviting glow, while an Eco-Fire burning on the clean fuel of methylated spirits adds to the warm and cosy effect.

4 We sourced bar stools featuring an Egyptian-style design from a secondhand store and, after spray-painting them black, cut them down to size to use as low seating and side tables for flexible entertaining. Soft furnishings including a Persian-inspired rug and colourful cushions in rich, earthy tones were added for cosiness and comfort.

5 For a lively, celebratory effect an authentic camel blanket was hung around the pergola. A hammock—selected for its similar style and knotting—was also hung, creating a relaxed feel.

6 Decorative glassware, brass vases and peacock feathers were introduced to the table setting for colour and overall exotic appeal.

7 An ornate low-voltage metal lantern was used as a centrepiece in the pergola, completing the Egyptian look.

JAMIE BROUGHT HOME:

- Brass incense burner
- Hanging brass lamp
- Decorative camel blanket

Look out for similar Egyptian and Egyptian-inspired items at markets and stores in your area.

a balinese pavilion

Lush, serene and tranquil, Bali is truly an island paradise. Surrounded by coral reefs, its coastal beaches give way to volcanic mountains in the centre, while in the lower foothills tropical rainforests and rice terraces dominate the landscape.

This tiny island is so inspiring—with its vibrant, fragrant flowers, abundance of tropical fruit, exotic plants and spectacular scenery all around, it is virtually impossible not to slow down and soak up the atmosphere.

One of Indonesia's 33 provinces, Bali has a population of around 3 million and is the first of the Lesser Sunda Islands, lying between Java and Lombok. Although it is just 112km north to south and 153km east to west. The climate is hot and humid, with an average temperature of 28°C, although the higher altitudes can be considerably cooler. Like most tropical climates, there are two main seasons—the rainy season, from October to March, and the dry season for the rest of the year.

Bali is so much more than Kuta Beach and the popular tourist areas surrounding it. Ceremony, religion and tradition play a major role in Balinese life. The vast majority of the population practise the Balinese Hindu religion. With its roots in Indian Hinduism, Buddhism and other ancient, local traditions, the cultural focus is on art, ritual and the fundamental belief that every element of nature is a reflection of the gods. Offerings of food and flowers left at temple sites are commonplace and statues, sculpture and artworks rich in religious symbology are scattered everywhere, from public gardens to private homes and compounds.

Bali's tropical climate makes it the perfect place for indoor—outdoor living. A traditional Balinese house is more of a family compound, consisting of several pavilions or huts that each have a different purpose, such as dining room, sleeping room, mens' accommodation, womens' accommodation and family meeting room, as well as a family temple and garden courtyard.

The Balinese have an innate sense of harmony and regard their homes and gardens as an extension of themselves. Before building, they must observe a set of rules, known as *Asta Kosala Kosali*, to ensure synchronicity between the body and the environment. Completely attuned with nature, Balinese homes are peaceful and serene, flowing seamlessly in and out of their natural surroundings as if they've been sculpted from the very land they are built on. And the gardens are no exception—curved pathways, stepping stones and linking bridges allow for slow meandering and thoughtful meditation; trickling water, bowls of water lilies (*Nymphaea*) and a statue of Buddha amongst tropical plants create a tranquil space; and intricate stone carvings and painted wooden gates combine with lanterns and vibrant temple flags to bring the garden to life. The Balinese ability to connect so deeply with their environment is nothing short of inspiring.

inspired design ideas

PAVILION OR BALINESE HUT

With its thatched roof, the Balinese hut, or pavilion, is an essential ingredient for a Balinese-themed garden. Visually, it will look enticing and add an exotic, natural feel. On a practical level, depending on your climate, it will help to extend the use of your garden year-round.

WATER FEATURE

Water features are often a central theme in Balinese gardens. The sound of water trickling lazily over natural stones and statues is so tranquil, it instantly soothes and relaxes. Also, in a hot climate it's great for cooling the air.

TROPICAL PLANTS

The typical Balinese garden is abundant with lush, tropical greenery. Ferns, frangipanis and palms all conjure up a distinctive Bali style. The traveller's palm (*Ravenala madagascariensis*) is a great addition to a tropical garden as it collects water and stores it in its leaves so that it can use it when needed.

STONE CARVINGS

The Balinese are experts in stone carvings and just one simple carving can make all the difference in your garden. Aside from adding texture and interest to your garden, the simplicity and themes of the carvings also set a peaceful, serene tone to the space.

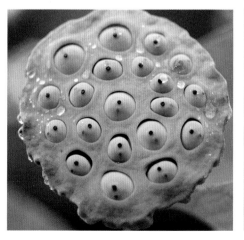

bali at home

The owners of this newly-built home had recently moved here in search of warmer weather. They were passionate about the tropics, particularly Bali with its thatched-roof pavilions and indoor—outdoor lifestyle. A contemporary, tropical environment was also their ideal garden setting for their upcoming wedding.

The house already had some good basic ingredients for a Balinese-style garden. The back of the house had a covered outdoor space stepping down into an overgrown lawn, with a pool at the end of the property. The potential was there—inspiration and design were all that was needed to turn this space into a romantic Balinese outdoor room.

We started by clearing the space in the covered outdoor deck. An existing spa, which took up a lot of room, was moved to the side of house for privacy and worked into the design of the garden, surrounded with ginger (*Alpinia*) and heliconias (*Heliconia*). Free of the spa, the deck—which would style up beautifully with Balinese-style furnishings—now became a spacious entrance and overview to the garden.

To frame the lawn area, we created a serpent-shaped paved edge which curved around the garden from the base of the steps to the pool. On each side of the garden, along the fence boundaries, additional palms (*Dypsis decaryi*), gingers (*Alpinia*), canna lilies (*Canna* 'Pretoria') and philodendrons (*Philodendron* 'Xanadu') were brought in to screen and bulk up the foliage. A small, pebbled area containing a water bowl with water lilies (*Nymphaea*) in the centre added a sense of harmony.

The central focus of this garden is the pool area, so here we created a water feature using a stunning stone carving that I brought back from Bali. To do this we built a steel frame, clad it with fibre-cement sheeting and fixed the carving on to it. We then redirected the flow of water from the pool filter up the back of the sculpture.

The fences surrounding the pool were all clad in Natureed to add to the tropical feel. On either side of the stone relief we planted two mature traveller's palms (*Ravenala madagascariensis*)—symbolic of two lovers kissing for the first time and just what I needed as a final romantic touch.

Next to the pool we built a Balinese thatched-roof pavilion for a relaxation and entertainment area. Timber batton screening gives it privacy and a cosy feel. The deck underneath the pavilion spills out to the pool's edge and I designed two large daybeds for ultimate luxury and serenity. Lady palms (*Rhapis excelsa*) growing through two man-made holes form a vertical garden. Stepping down from the pavilion are large, timber pontoon steppers embedded in a pebble ground cover and a paved barbeque area. The overall effect is a relaxed environment that flows easily, making it the perfect entertainer on those balmy, tropical nights.

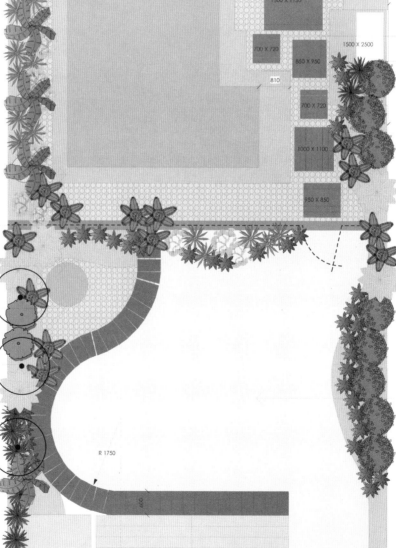

Note: Plans may vary from design to construction

2100MM LONG FIBREGLASS WATER
RESERVOIR WITH AS SELECTED DRAIN
AND PEBBLE OVER

20MM DEEP COPPER CHANNEL TO DRAIN
WATER FROM RESERVOIR TO POOL

STONE PANEL WATER FEATURE TO BE
CONNECTED TO POOL FILTER SYSTEM.
STONE PANELS FIXED TO STEEL POSTS
TO ENGINEERS DETAIL

PEBBLE MULCH AROUND POOL (36 SQ.M)

EXISTING SCREEN
AROUND POOL
EQUIPMENT TO
REMAIN

TIMBER PLATFORM (12 SQ.M)
WITH TIMBER BENCH
SEATING AND THATCH HUT
OVER

TIMBER SCREEN
AROUND 2 SIDES
OF PLATFORM

EXISTING BAMBOO
PLANTING ALONG
BOUNDARY FENCE
TO REMAIN

TIMBER PONTOON
STEPPERS—REFER
TO DETAIL

Strelitzia nicolai
PLANTED IN 5
FEATURE POTS
ALONG
BOUNDARY FENCE

AS SELECTED
BBQ ON PAVED
PLATFORM,
MASONRY WALL
BEHIND CLAD IN
STONE AS
SELECTED

EXISTING POOL
AND COPING TO
REMAIN

EXISTING POOL
FENCE AND GATE
TO REMAIN

STONE WATER
BOWL NESTLED
AMONGST FOLIAGE

PEBBLE (9 SQ.M)

APPROX. LOCATIONS
OF EXISTING PALMS
PLANTED ALONG
BOUNDARY

NEW LAWN (49 SQ.M)

PAVED EDGE TO
PEBBLE AREA AND
AS LANDING AT
BOTTOM OF EXISTING
STEPS

EXISTING SPA TO BE
RELOCATED TO SIDE
OF HOUSE

Previous page—clockwise from left:

- Typical of Balinese garden design, the timber deck of the pavilion stretches right to the water's edge, creating a seamless transition between the pool and entertaining area. Large timber steppers surrounded by pebbles continue this effect through the garden.

- Tropical plants such as canna lilies (*Canna* 'Pretoria') and tree ferns (*Cyathea australis*) were used throughout the garden not only to replicate the Balinese style, but because they grow so well in the climate the garden is situated in.

This page—clockwise from bottom left:

- Dense planting adds to the garden's tropical feel.

- A groundcover of Rhoeo (*Tradescantia spathacea)* adds interest between the steppers.

- This carved-stone Balinese relief introduces an authentic focal point to the design. Re-purposed as a water feature, the peaceful imagery and running water create a calming atmosphere.

- The serpentine-shaped garden edge doubles as a pathway leading from the garden to the pool.

Facing page:

- Water features are an important element in Balinese-style gardens. A simple bowl filled with water and lilies (*Nymphaea*) is easy to install and instantly creates a tranquil feel.

design key

Create your own Balinese-style outdoor living space by incorporating some of the planting, material, furniture and accessories ideas we came up with for our garden. Introduce new elements to existing features to create a central focus and an inviting area in which to entertain and relax.

PLANTS

TREES
- *Cyathea australis* ROUGH TREE FERN (4)
- *Dypsis decaryi* TRIANGLE PALM
- *Plumeria obtusa* WHITE FRANGIPANI
- *Ravenala madagascariensis* TRAVELLER'S PALM

SHRUBS
- *Canna* 'Pretoria' VARIEGATED CANNA LILY (1, 2)
- *Cordyline fruticosa* 'Pink Diamond' PINK DIAMOND TI PLANT
- *Crinum pedunculatum* SWAMP LILY
- *Doryanthes excelsa* GYMEA LILY
- *Dracaena reflexa* 'Variegata' VAR. SONG OF INDIA
- *Furcraea foetida* 'Mediopicta' VAR. MAURITIUS HEMP
- *Gardenia* 'True Love' GARDENIA
- *Hedychium* 'Luna Moth' LUNA MOTH GINGER
- *Philodendron* 'Xanadu' XANADU PHILODENDRON
- *Rhapis excelsa* LADY PALM
- *Strelitzia nicolai* GIANT BIRD OF PARADISE
- *Viburnum odoratissimum* 'Emerald Lustre' EMERALD LUSTRE VIBURNUM

CLIMBERS
- *Mandevilla sanderi* CHILEAN JASMINE

GROUNDCOVERS
- *Liriope muscari* LILY TURF
- *Tradescantia spathacea* RHOEO (3)

WATER PLANTS
- *Nymphaea* cvs WATER LILY

MATERIALS

WALLS
- Timber batten screens provide privacy for the pavilion.
- The fences surrounding the pool were clad in Natureed, covering existing boundary fences (5).

FLOORS
- The floor of the pavilion was lined with timber.
- A mix of pebbles and timber pontoon steppers surrounds the entertaining area (3).
- The large section of lawn in the centre of the garden was framed by a serpentine-shaped edging of concrete pavers on one side. This also doubles as a garden path.
- Concrete pavers form the ground plane of the barbecue area (3).

OVERHEAD
- A Balinese-style thatched roof was used to cover the pavilion (1, 4).

FEATURES
- An authentic hand-carved stone wall was re-purposed to create a water feature (2).
- A stone bowl was filled with water plants as a feature in the garden bed.

FURNITURE AND ACCESSORIES

1 Colourful mats and bench cushions are the ideal accessory for a Balinese garden. They not only introduce a lively element to the garden, but also provide comfort and a relaxed look and feel.

2 We added built-in bench seating for easy entertaining. Bench seating is a great idea as it can also include under-seat storage for easy access to cushions and rugs. The timber table and chairs are reflective of Balinese style and comfort and will weather well, making it suitable for all seasons.

3 Prayer flags in traditional Balinese colours create a celebratory look and feel.

4 Water features are a common theme in Balinese gardens. Here we sourced an oversized ceramic bowl and filled it with water lilies (*Nymphaea*) as a permanent fixture in the garden. This will add to the calm, relaxed ambience of the garden.

5, 6 & 7 Candles create a warm and inviting mood in the garden. Here we used candle holders made out of carved stone to tie-in with the carved-stone pool feature, carved wooden statue and overall theme of the garden. Sea shells dotted around enhance the relaxed, resort-style feel.

JAMIE BROUGHT HOME:

▥ Carved stone wall (which we turned into a water feature)

▥ Prayer flags

▥ Wooden yogi in prayer position

Look out for similar Balinese and Balinese-inspired items at markets and stores in your area.

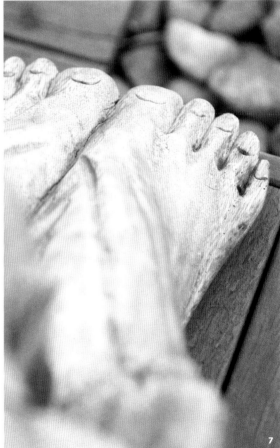

a french conservatory

With their catwalks and cafes, galleries and gardens, France and Paris are synonymous with culture, style and romance.

Situated in the heart of Europe, France is arguably the historic pulse of European high culture and design. From as early as the 17th century, the French people have been at the forefront of innovation in art, architecture, cuisine, fashion, philosophy, theatre, literature, politics, landscape and design. Their influence has been significant and lasting, and garden design is no exception.

Lying in the southern part of the temperate zone, the traditional French garden is one of precision, geometric symmetry and romantic grandeur. Following the French invasions of Italy in the early 16th century, French garden design began to display a strong Italian influence. However, while the Italians built on the lower slopes of hills near cities, the French built on agricultural plains where there was more opportunity for expansive designs. Following a period of experimentation in artistic form, the French emerged from the Renaissance with the distinctive baroque style that became the foundation of formal garden design worldwide.

Composed of elaborate parterres, hedges and axes radiating from a central building or pavilion, and punctuated with statues, fountains and canals, baroque French gardens were designed for nobility and show—grand artworks to be viewed from above. However, ever since Louis XIV opened Paris's oldest and most famous garden— the Tuileries—to the public in the 1660s, they were also designed as places for people to meet and interact, with benches, wide alleys, smaller spaces to gather and a *potager* (vegetable plot).

The most influential landscape designer of the 17th century was André Le Nôtre, who, having studied the laws of perspective and optics with the studio painter François Vouet, was both visionary artist and passionate horticulturalist. As chief gardener of the Tuileries, Le Nôtre redesigned the garden and its central axis to become the grand axis of Paris, running as it does today to the Arc de Triomphe. He also designed the grand gardens of Versailles and Vaux-le-Vicomte.

While 17th-century French gardens displayed a sense of control and manipulation of nature, the 18th century gave way to a freer, more natural view. By the 19th century French gardens were strategically planned around interesting walking paths, with the addition of flowers. Famous gardens of these times include Giverny, the gardens of renowned French painter Claude Monet.

Not fond of constrained formal gardens, Monet applied his artistic eye to create a garden of perspective and symmetry, arranging flowers according to colour and leaving them to grow freely in a more natural, cottage style. On the other side of the road from his flower garden, Monet created a Japanese-inspired water garden based on asymmetrical shapes, curves and elements of reflection—shaping the natural landscape in order to capture its exact likeness in his paintings.

Historically, French gardens have represented the place where art, science, mathematics and nature intersect with the human experience. Contemporary French artist, scientist and botanist Patrick Blanc continues this tradition with his innovative creation—the Vertical Garden (Le Mur Végétal). Growing low-light foliage plants on a frame of metal, PVC and non-biodegradable felt without soil, Blanc has revolutionised traditional horizontal gardening as we know it. Passionate about the science of plants, as well as their architecture and texture, Blanc strives to create living artworks that bring nature into the urban environment—on the walls of city buildings, in shopping centres and offices—to connect people with plants in an inspiring way.

inspired design ideas

CONSERVATORY

A popular feature of the French formal garden, the conservatory or pavilion is a place for people to gather—to socialise, take respite from the weather and to view the garden in comfort.

THE VERTICAL GARDEN

Patrick Blanc's creation of the Vertical Garden has become popular worldwide, transforming the possibilities of what a garden can be and offering remarkable solutions for public buildings and inner city and small-space gardens. With a focus on texture and form, these gardens are truly inspirational.

COLOURFUL COTTAGE FLOWERS

As in the less formal gardens of Monet, beds planted with a myriad of colourful flowers grouped together freely in asymmetrical form add a charming touch to a French-style garden.

PLEACHED TREES

A popular practice in French gardens and street planting, pleaching—clearing trees of their lower branches and pruning the canopy to form a continuous elevated hedge—allows foliage to grow in the foreground, while framing an unobstructed view beyond.

CHANDELIER

Taking the indoors outside, and drawing inspiration from the traditionally grand baroque gardens of high-society France, the chandelier epitomises French opulence, charm and sculptural beauty.

france at home

With just a few existing trees on a level block, this garden provided little in the way of interesting features to draw design inspiration from. Digging deeper to discover that the owners have family in France, however, was all the inspiration I needed.

To get started, I drew upon some of my favourite French gardens—including the grand gardens of Versailles, Monet's flower garden and Patrick Blanc's Vertical Gardens—to envisage the possibilities of where this blank canvas could go. I decided to incorporate influences from each of my favourite styles to create a contemporary version of the quintessential French garden.

One of the elements that impresses me most about the traditional baroque style is the creation of multiple spaces for people to gather within the garden. With this in mind, I based the design around a central dining area and conservatory, with an additional timber deck and seating area for flexible entertaining and relaxation.

A timber deck, which also doubles as a bench seat, was built from the back of the house to provide a sunny morning dining area with a breakfast setting from which to view the garden beyond. A central path bordered either side by a rambling Monet-style mass planting of flowers, herbs, vegetables and trees leads to an arbour framed by a high pleached hedge of magnolia (*Magnolia grandiflora* 'Exmouth').

Constructed from decorative lattice and painted in a green-tinted limewash, the arbour divides the cottage-style garden from the more formal paved area. Lined by a screen planting of sweet viburnum (*Viburnum odoratissimum*) on either side, the single vertical-line planting is designed to visually elongate the paved space and direct your eye through to the central conservatory. The cream colour of the concrete pavers and the bed of decomposed granite, white crushed quartz and green recycled glass surrounding the pavilion further enhance this effect by keeping the garden looking light and bright.

The conservatory itself is octagonal and features open-sided entrances on two opposite sides. The remaining six sides feature square lattice panels with inserts of light blue and pink transparent film over glass and a Perspex skylight in the roof to encourage more light. Drawing upon the opulence and charm of 17th-century French baroque style, the pavilion is decorated with a 120-year-old French chandelier in blue and white blown glass and two pieces of antique fabric—sourced from an original Louis XIV couch—mounted between two pieces of glass and hung like a picture in an ornate gilded frame. A Napoleon chair, decorative glassware, soft curtains and colourful cushions complete the look, making this intimate entertaining and relaxation space both comfortable and inviting. From inside the conservatory, one can see back through the pleached hedge to the Monet-style garden and forward through to the Patrick Blanc-inspired vertical garden, which was pre-planted six months in advance before being hung here in vertical form.

Planted with textural ornamental grasses and foliage plants, the vertical garden makes a stunning feature at the far end of the yard. Timber bench seats surrounded by a planting of purple fountain grass (*Pennisetum advena* 'Rubra') in front and on either side of the vertical garden create an additional area for entertaining and relaxation in the dappled shade of the existing mulberry trees.

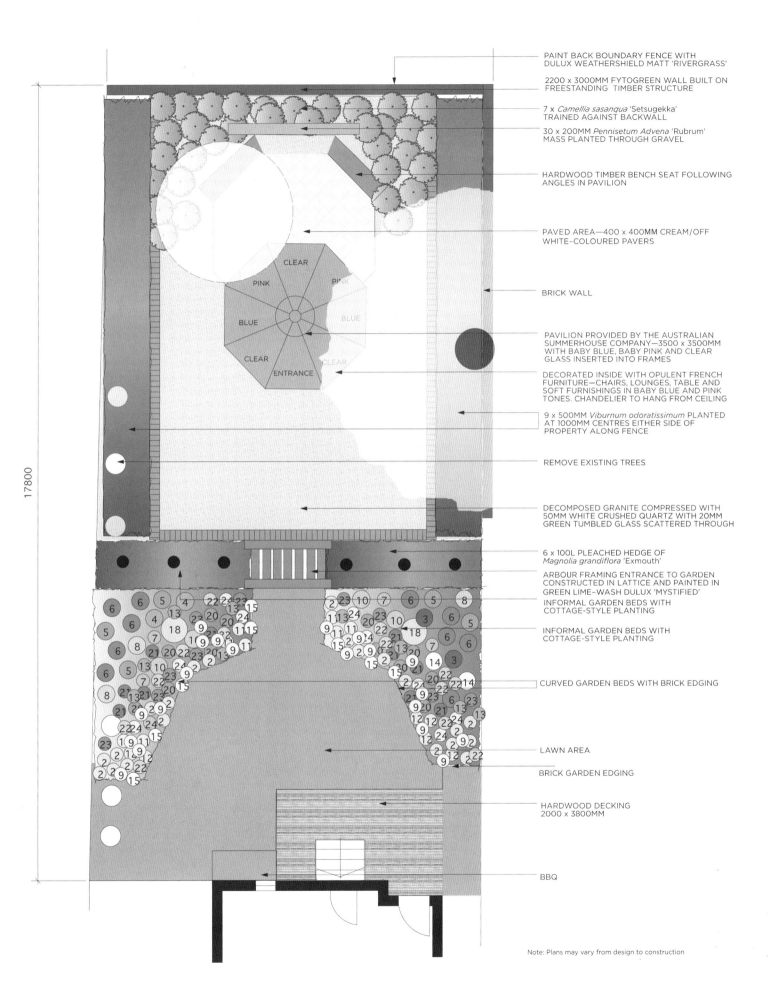

PAINT BACK BOUNDARY FENCE WITH
DULUX WEATHERSHIELD MATT 'RIVERGRASS'

2200 x 3000MM FYTOGREEN WALL BUILT ON
FREESTANDING TIMBER STRUCTURE

7 x *Camellia sasanqua* 'Setsugekka'
TRAINED AGAINST BACKWALL

30 x 200MM *Pennisetum Advena* 'Rubrum'
MASS PLANTED THROUGH GRAVEL

HARDWOOD TIMBER BENCH SEAT FOLLOWING
ANGLES IN PAVILION

PAVED AREA—400 x 400MM CREAM/OFF
WHITE-COLOURED PAVERS

BRICK WALL

PAVILION PROVIDED BY THE AUSTRALIAN
SUMMERHOUSE COMPANY—3500 x 3500MM
WITH BABY BLUE, BABY PINK AND CLEAR
GLASS INSERTED INTO FRAMES

DECORATED INSIDE WITH OPULENT FRENCH
FURNITURE—CHAIRS, LOUNGES, TABLE AND
SOFT FURNISHINGS IN BABY BLUE AND PINK
TONES. CHANDELIER TO HANG FROM CEILING

9 x 500MM *Viburnum odoratissimum* PLANTED
AT 1000MM CENTRES EITHER SIDE OF
PROPERTY ALONG FENCE

REMOVE EXISTING TREES

DECOMPOSED GRANITE COMPRESSED WITH
50MM WHITE CRUSHED QUARTZ WITH 20MM
GREEN TUMBLED GLASS SCATTERED THROUGH

6 x 100L PLEACHED HEDGE OF
Magnolia grandiflora 'Exmouth'

ARBOUR FRAMING ENTRANCE TO GARDEN
CONSTRUCTED IN LATTICE AND PAINTED IN
GREEN LIME–WASH DULUX 'MYSTIFIED'

INFORMAL GARDEN BEDS WITH
COTTAGE-STYLE PLANTING

INFORMAL GARDEN BEDS WITH
COTTAGE-STYLE PLANTING

CURVED GARDEN BEDS WITH BRICK EDGING

LAWN AREA

BRICK GARDEN EDGING

HARDWOOD DECKING
2000 x 3800MM

BBQ

17800

CLEAR
PINK PINK
BLUE BLUE
CLEAR CLEAR
ENTRANCE

Note: Plans may vary from design to construction

a french conservatory **63**

Previous page:

• Against the backdrop of the vertical garden the built-in timber bench seating makes a cosy spot to relax at the rear of the garden. The benches are softened by the addition of cushions.

This page—clockwise from bottom left:

• Purple fountain grass (*Pennisetum advena* 'Rubra')—planted amongst herbs and flowers in the Monet-style garden—adds texture and colour to the planting scheme.

• Alternating tinted windows in soft pink and blue create gentle colour inside the conservatory and add soft light day and night.

• A touch of French grandeur, the antique chandelier casts a romantic evening glow. Combined with soft furnishings to create a luxurious and relaxing atmosphere, this is the ultimate outdoor room experience.

Facing page:

• Four pleached magnolia trees (*Magnolia grandiflora* 'Exmouth') flank either side of the arbour. As they grow they will form a high hedge; their pleached trunks still allowing for a view of the garden beyond.

Clockwise from far left:

- The arbour is made from timber and square lattice panels and finished with a light-green tinted lime-wash. Nestled in the rambling Monet-style cottage garden it divides the garden areas and acts as an entrance to the more formal-style paved entertaining area.

- Two authentic antique Louis XIV French tapestries were each mounted between two panels of glass and framed with a gilt timber frame to mirror the traditional furnishings. The tapestry can be viewed from both inside and outside the pavilion.

- The pavilion is a mix of traditional and contemporary styling. Traditional in its form, two open-sided entrances draw the eye from the arbour through the pavilion to the vertical garden at the rear. Overhead, the internal exposed beams of the octagonal roof and external shingles are all painted dove-grey. An antique French chandelier adds opulence and charm to the space, and a Perspex skylight allows for maximum sunlight to peep through.

design key

Create your own French-style outdoor living space by incorporating some of the planting, material, furniture and accessories ideas we came up with for our garden. Blending different styles to create an overall look can easily be achieved by creating different 'zones' within your design.

PLANTS

TREES
- *Fortunella japonica* 'Marumi' ROUND CUMQUAT
- *Magnolia grandiflora* 'Exmouth' EXMOUTH MAGNOLIA

SHRUBS, GRASSES, VEGETABLES AND FLOWERS
- *Acorus gramineus* 'Variegatus' VARIEGATED JAPANESE RUSH
- *Argyranthemum* 'Blazer Rose' BLAZER ROSE DAISY (4)
- *Aster ericoides* 'Pink Star' PINK STAR ASTER
- *Brassica oleracea* cvs ORNAMENTAL CABBAGE (1)
- *Camellia sasanqua* 'Setsugekka' SETSUGEKKA CAMELLIA
- *Cerastium tomentosum* SNOW IN SUMMER
- *Cynara scolymus* GLOBE ARTICHOKE
- *Lavandula stoechas* 'Lavender Lace' LAVENDER LACE LAVENDER
- *Limonium perezii* SEAFOAM STATICE
- *Liriope muscari* LILY TURF
- *Osteospermum* 'Lemon Mist' LEMON MIST DAISY (4)
- *Osteospermum* 'White Mist' WHITE MIST DAISY (4)
- *Pennisetum advena* 'Rubra' PURPLE FOUNTAIN GRASS (3)
- *Plectranthus argentatus* SILVER SPUR FLOWER
- *Salvia* 'Anthony Parker' ANTHONY PARKER SAGE
- *Salvia greggii* 'Lara' LARA AUTUMN SAGE
- *Salvia guaranitica* 'Tequila Blue' TEQUILA BLUE SAGE
- *Strobilanthes anisophyllus* GOLDFUSSIA
- *Strobilanthes gossypinus* PERSIAN SHIELD
- *Viburnum odoratissimum* SWEET VIBURNUM

MATERIALS

WALLS
- Vertical garden panel attached to a free-standing timber structure set 2 metres in from the boundary fence.
- Timber frame arbour and conservatory made from treated pine and square lattice (1), painted in a light green limewash. The conservatory walls are inset with pink- and blue-transparent film over glass panels (5).

FLOORS
- Hardwood timber deck stained with natural-coloured decking oil.
- Compacted decomposed granite with green recycled glass and white crushed quartz scattered through (4).
- Cream-coloured concrete pavers line the floor of the entertaining area and pathways.
- Brick edging made from recycled mixed kiln-dried bricks lines the perimeter of garden.

OVERHEAD
- The pavilion roof is made out of timber slats with painted fibre cement shingles and features a clear Perspex skylight (3).

FEATURES
- Built-in bench seating made from treated pine frames and hardwood timber slats between the arbour frame and in front of the vertical wall (2).

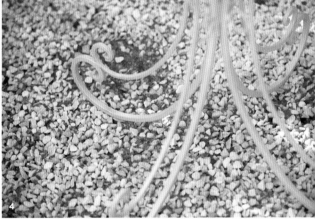

FURNITURE
AND ACCESSORIES

1 These decorative outdoor glasses and jug teamed with a second-hand glass bowl filled with flowers bring old-world Parisian charm to the setting. The stainless steel table contrasts with the traditional style of the conservatory and other French-style furnishings and accessories.

2 Traditional French bone cutlery is laid on top of simple linen napkins.

3 Sourced from France, this 120-year-old glass-blown chandelier makes a stunning central feature in the conservatory, adding grace, elegance and typical French chic.

4 This reproduction of a traditional Napolean armchair has been left with its original calico lining exposed to create an interesting mix of traditional and contemporary styles.

5 Cushions scattered on seating throughout the garden feature fabric with a metallic sheen to tie in with the gilt armchair and ornate styling.

6 Dove-grey translucent fabric panels with a faint damask pattern for texture take on the colours of the tinted windows in the conservatory.

7 A painted-white wrought iron cafe-style setting blends beautifully with the white crushed quartz and green tumbled glass underfoot.

JAMIE BROUGHT HOME:

- Louis XIV antique fabric
- 120-year-old glass-blown chandelier

Look out for similar French and French-inspired items at markets and stores in your area.

a south african hideaway

Spanning the southernmost tip of the African continent, South Africa is famous for its plants and wildlife, boasting some of the best botanical gardens in the world.

Home to some 44 million people, it is also the largest African country, with the most dynamic economy on the continent. Due to its ethnically diverse population it is often referred to by its people as the 'Rainbow Nation', with 11 official languages. Culturally, music and dance feature prominently and perhaps due to the wild terrain and wide-open spaces, South Africans have an impressive respect for nature and wildlife. I've never seen sunsets like those I've experienced in South Africa—they make me feel like I'm the only person on earth and the colours are phenomenal.

Travelling west to east, South Africa borders Namibia and Botswana, Zimbabwe and Mozambique to the east, before curving around Swaziland and completely surrounding a small, mountainous country called Lesotho in its interior. Its long coastline travels south for over 2500km from its desert border with Namibia on the Atlantic coast, around the tip of Africa and then north to the border with subtropical Mozambique on the Indian Ocean.

Although the country is officially classified as semi-arid, there are significant variations in both climate and topography. Inland is the Karoo plateau, known for its rocky hills and mountains and sparsely populated scrubland. Here, it is very dry and gets more so as you travel north into the North West province, towards the Kalahari desert. Extremely hot in summer, it can be icy in winter, although it rarely snows.

In contrast, the eastern coastline is lush and well-watered, with a tropical feel. On the southern coast it is less tropical but very green and the southwestern corner is almost Mediterranean in climate, with wet winters and hot, dry summers. Similar to our own climate in Australia, it's no wonder so many South African native plants thrive in our country.

The raw beauty of South Africa is spectacular—for me it's a sensory overload. Despite the extremes in climate it is always putting on a diverse and abundant display of wildlife and plants. Large areas of land are dedicated to nature and wild animals such as elephants, giraffes, hippos, lions and zebras right on its doorstep. Around 10 per cent of the world's flowering species are found here and it is the only country in the world with an entire plant kingdom inside its borders. This is a country that not only respects nature, but is both humbled by it and proud of it and, in my mind, it's this reverence for the natural environment that has had the most influence on the gardens of the region.

inspired design ideas

NATURAL OBJECTS

Take a look around your environment—almost any object found in nature can become a feature in your garden. The more you can incorporate natural objects into your garden and living spaces, the more you are bringing the outside in and making the natural environment a part of your daily life.

STACKED STONE

The use of stacked stone can create drama in a landscape. As a decorative, sculptural element, it retains nature as the central focus. Used practically, such as for edging or walls, it's a clever way to integrate function with the natural environment.

DROUGHT-RESISTANT PLANTS

South African native plants are perfect for the hot, dry Australian climate. What I love about drought-resistant plants is not only their ability to hold water and use it as needed, but also that they require less water in general. It makes them ideal plants for low-maintenance gardeners.

WOODEN CARVINGS

Traditional wooden carvings are the perfect way to introduce a slice of history and culture into your garden. As an ornamental feature, the symbolism and unique design of a carving can be the final touch that brings your outdoor room to life.

MUD-RENDERED WALLS

Earthy, warm and very African, mud-rendered-style walls give any space a tribal, raw look and feel. Taking us right back to nature, they are the ultimate in creating an African mood.

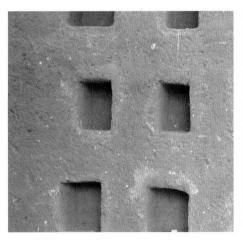

south africa at home

Despite having never travelled there themselves, the owners of this suburban home had a strong penchant for all things African. The many native artefacts and decorations they had in their home already lent themselves to an African-inspired theme, so it was easy to follow this through with the garden design.

The owners wanted a drought-tolerant, low-maintenance garden with no lawn at all. The trick to realising this was to avoid thirsty plants and minimise evaporation, which we achieved by using a combination of gravels, recycled timber, stone and South African natives for the ground plane and stacked-stone edging—inspired by the terrace gardens I saw in South Africa—around the garden beds. The blend of different textures underfoot kept the space interesting and gave it an untamed, natural look.

The garden already had a freestanding fireplace and as this is often the centre for many outdoor gatherings in their home, we wanted to maintain its central focus. I altered it slightly, using the base to create a large fire-pot and surrounding it with stacked stones for insulation and thematic placement. We then incorporated it into the design by extending the existing deck area into an organic shape and adding hand-rendered built-in seating in mud-brick style to encourage a place for gathering. The original balustrade around the deck was removed and replaced with a continuous set of steps to open up the space and connect with the rest of garden.

Next, we worked with existing material to add to the tribal feel of the garden. The vertical post supporting the garage was clad with natural tree branches and surrounded by stones and boulders. In the garage itself, we fitted an old timber bench and used a natural red stone paver for the floor. Brushbox screening for the walls gave us the ideal backdrop for African art pieces from my trip.

Proteas (*Protea cynaroides* 'Little Prince') and leucadendrons (*Leucadendron salignum* 'Red Devil' and *Leucadendron* 'Safari Sunset') were planted around the boundary of the garden, forming the bulk of shrubs. For accents we used succulents—variegated jade plant (*Crassula ovata* 'Hummel's Sunset') and blue chalk sticks (*Senecio serpens*)—and jelly bean plants (*Sedum rubrotinctum* and *Sedum pachyphyllum*) for ground covers. Fountain rush (*Elegia capensis*), cape rush (*Chondropetalum tectorum*) and proteas (*Protea cynaroides* 'Little Prince') were planted around the water feature. Most of these plants are native to South Africa and are also very suitable for the Australian climate.

A water feature can be a great addition to a garden to add movement and life and attract birds and other wildlife. Inspired by a feature I'd seen in South Africa, I roughly sketched tree branches into a slab of aerated concrete, then turned this into a series of carved grooves, allowing water to meander through and spill gently into a reservoir below. We then ground all the corners off the masonry and bagged and rendered it in a red earth ochre to pick up the colours of the African soil. The grooves remained white to add more definition. To add visual depth, we stacked natural stones into giant, man-size cones, then up-lit them to add a sense of drama and art into the landscape. Natural looking mud-brick style bench seats were added nearby as a quiet place to sit and soak up the surrounding nature and wildlife. The final result—a functional outdoor space with a raw, African appeal.

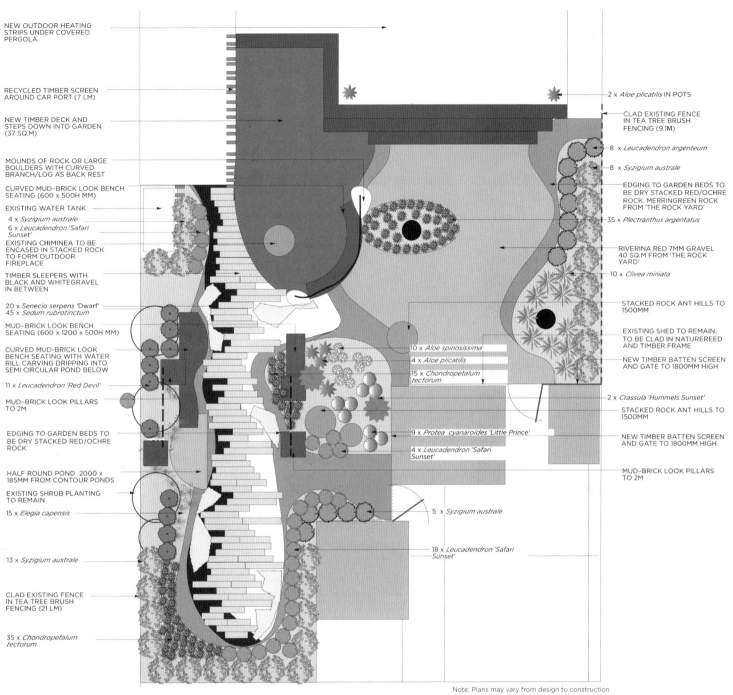

NEW OUTDOOR HEATING STRIPS UNDER COVERED PERGOLA

RECYCLED TIMBER SCREEN AROUND CAR PORT (7 LM)

NEW TIMBER DECK AND STEPS DOWN INTO GARDEN (37 SQ.M)

MOUNDS OF ROCK OR LARGE BOULDERS WITH CURVED BRANCH/LOG AS BACK REST

CURVED MUD-BRICK LOOK BENCH SEATING (600 x 500H MM)

EXISTING WATER TANK

4 x *Syzigium australe*
6 x *Leucadendron 'Safari Sunset'*

EXISTING CHIMINEA TO BE ENCASED IN STACKED ROCK TO FORM OUTDOOR FIREPLACE

TIMBER SLEEPERS WITH BLACK AND WHITEGRAVEL IN BETWEEN

20 x *Senecio serpens 'Dwarf'*
45 x *Sedum rubrotinctum*

MUD-BRICK LOOK BENCH SEATING (600 x 1200 x 500H MM)

CURVED MUD-BRICK LOOK BENCH SEATING WITH WATER RILL CARVING DRIPPING INTO SEMI CIRCULAR POND BELOW

11 x *Leucadendron 'Red Devil'*

MUD-BRICK LOOK PILLARS TO 2M

EDGING TO GARDEN BEDS TO BE DRY STACKED RED/OCHRE ROCK

HALF ROUND POND 2000 x 185MM FROM CONTOUR PONDS

EXISTING SHRUB PLANTING TO REMAIN

15 x *Elegia capensis*

13 x *Syzigium australe*

CLAD EXISTING FENCE IN TEA TREE BRUSH FENCING (21 LM)

35 x *Chondropetalum tectorum*

2 x *Aloe plicatilis* IN POTS

CLAD EXISTING FENCE IN TEA TREE BRUSH FENCING (9.1M)

8 x *Leucadendron argenteum*

8 x *Syzigium australe*

EDGING TO GARDEN BEDS TO BE DRY STACKED RED/OCHRE ROCK. MERRINGREEN ROCK FROM 'THE ROCK YARD'

35 x *Plectranthus argentatus*

RIVERINA RED 7MM GRAVEL 40 SQ.M FROM 'THE ROCK YARD'

10 x *Clivea miniata*

STACKED ROCK ANT HILLS TO 1500MM

EXISTING SHED TO REMAIN. TO BE CLAD IN NATUREREED AND TIMBER FRAME

NEW TIMBER BATTEN SCREEN AND GATE TO 1800MM HIGH

2 x *Crassula 'Hummels Sunset'*

STACKED ROCK ANT HILLS TO 1500MM

NEW TIMBER BATTEN SCREEN AND GATE TO 1800MM HIGH

MUD-BRICK LOOK PILLARS TO 2M

10 x *Aloe spinosissima*

4 x *Aloe plicatilis*

15 x *Chondropetalum tectorum*

9 x *Protea cyanaroides 'Little Prince'*

4 x *Leucadendron 'Safari Sunset'*

5 x *Syzigium australe*

18 x *Leucadendron 'Safari Sunset'*

Note: Plans may vary from design to construction

Previous pages:

- Ochre-red scoria gravel is ideal for the ground plane of this garden because, unlike lawn, it requires no water, is low maintenance and its colour mirrors the South African landscape.

- When converting the existing carport into an outdoor dining area we clad the frames of the timber structure in birch branches and brush box to enhance the raw, natural mood of the garden.

This page—clockwise from top:

- The fireplace is a central focus of the garden, adding to the overall ambience and encouraging outdoor gatherings. The stacked stones surrounding the base continue the South African theme and provide essential insulation.

Facing page—from top:

- The mud-brick inspired bench seating provides multiple places within the garden to rest and relax. Here, the soft green foliage provides a stunning contrast to the ochre-colours in the seat, pot and cushions.

- The pathway through the garden is made from recycled timber sleepers and surrounded on either side by contrasting-coloured gravels and textural groundcovers. Pots along the path make interesting sculptural focal points.

Facing page—clockwise from bottom:

- Drought-hardy plants such as proteas (*Protea cynaroides* 'Little Prince'), jelly bean plants (*Sedum pachyphyllum* and *Sedum rubrotinctum*) and aloes (*Aloe plicatilis* and *Aloe* x *spinosissima*) are perfectly suited to both the South African and Australian climates. They also have lovely sculptural forms, which add interest to the overall design.

- The mud-brick inspired bench seating perfectly complements the natural materials palette of timber and stone.

This page—from top:

- Two mature jade plants were added for their drought-tolerant, hardy nature. Fitting in perfectly with the succulent planting theme, we planted one in a pot and one in the ground.

- Stacked stone mound sculptures made from locally quarried rock are set among the garden beds of native flowering shrubs like proteas (*Protea cynaroides* 'Little Prince') and Leucadendrons (*Leucadendron salignum* 'Red Devil' and *Leucadendron* 'Safari Sunset').

design key

Create your own African-style outdoor living space by incorporating some of the ideas we came up with for our garden. Shop in your own home and garden for items that might be useful outdoors, or might be modified or updated to fit your design theme.

PLANTS

TREES
- *Leucadendron argenteum* SILVER TREE

SHRUBS
- *Aloe plicatilis* FAN ALOE (2)
- *Aloe* x *spinosissima* GOLD TOOTH ALOE (3)
- *Clivia nobilis* CLIVIA
- *Crassula ovata* 'Hummel's Sunset' VARIEGATED JADE PLANT (4)
- *Leucadendron salignum* 'Red Devil' RED DEVIL
- *Leucadendron* 'Safari Sunset' SAFARI SUNSET
- *Protea cynaroides* 'Little Prince' LITTLE PRINCE (1)
- *Syzygium australe* SCRUB CHERRY

GROUNDCOVERS AND GRASSES
- *Chondropetalum tectorum* CAPE RUSH
- *Elegia capensis* FOUNTAIN RUSH
- *Plectranthus argentatus* SILVER SPUR FLOWER
- *Sedum pachyphyllum* BLUE JELLY BEANS
- *Sedum rubrotinctum* JELLY BEAN PLANT
- *Senecio serpens* BLUE CHALK STICKS

MATERIALS

WALLS
• Similar to Natureed, tea-tree brush fencing—
made up of small twigs and branches held
together with wire binding—was used to clad the
existing fences, shed and walls beneath the
carport. It provides a natural, informal look (1).

FLOORS
• Recycled timber sleepers are mixed with various
gravels to form the ground plane (2).
• The original timber deck was extended in an
organic shape.
• Red ochre-coloured pavers were used to line the
dining area.

FEATURES
• Natural rock was used for garden-bed edging
and as a sculptural element (3, 5).
• Aerated concrete with carved grooves, bagged
and rendered in a red-earth ochre colour, was
used to create built-in bench seats and water
feature (4).
• The vertical posts supporting the existing garage
were clad with natural tree branches and
surrounded by stones and boulders.

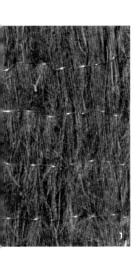

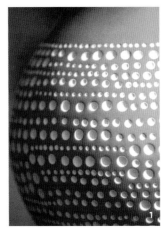

FURNITURE
AND ACCESSORIES

1 Accessories such as this terracotta pot continue the tones and textures of the stone-carved water feature that was custom designed for this garden.

2 & 7 Decorative outdoor table settings can add the finishing touch to your garden. We've used a traditional African mud cloth as a table runner, with grass-woven placemats and geometric-patterned cotton napkins for a raw and tribal look. Festive tea-glasses add colour and complement the rustic theme.

3 Bright cushions in African-inspired colours and patterns echo the earthy tones and texture of the African landscape, while bringing an element of softness and comfort to the garden.

4 Mud-rendered inspired seating was built in to create an instant, defined space for entertaining and get-togethers.

5 & 6 Sourced direct from South Africa, the traditional tribal sculptures and carved soapstone heads introduce an element of authenticity and character to the design.

8 A simple wooden table and bench chairs offers a perfect complement to the natural-style outdoor room and perfect canvas for a decoratively themed table setting.

JAMIE BROUGHT HOME:

- Black rhino sculpture
- Two carved tribal motifs
- Two African soapstone carved heads

Look out for similar South African and African-inspired items at markets and stores in your area.

an indian sanctuary

from the bustling metropolises of Delhi, Bombay and Calcutta, to the snow-capped peaks of the Himalayas in the north, the desert palaces of Rajasthan in the west, the holy waters of the Ganges in the east, and the backwaters of Kerala in the south, the streets of India are nothing short of intoxicating.

The moment you step onto them your senses are heightened and exhilarated. There's the flurry of colour, the jingling of bangles, the clanging of cow bells, the beeping of horns and the heady scent of incense, chai, samosas and sweets bubbling away in streetside stalls. With a population of over 1 billion, it's no surprise that Indian architecture and landscape design is all about creating a private sanctuary.

I'll never forget the first time I viewed the incredible island sanctuary of the Lake Palace Hotel in Udaipur—with its perfect white mirror image reflected back at me across Lake Pichola—it was breathtaking. Many of India's grand gardens have also had the same effect on me.

India has one of the oldest garden-design traditions in the world. Influences range from Roman and Persian garden customs, brought to India by Arab traders during the 10th and 11th centuries, to British colonisation in the mid-18th century. The most lasting influence emerged between the 16th and 18th centuries, during the time of the Islamic Mughal Empire. Influenced greatly in style by Persian and Timurid gardens, Mughal gardens characteristically feature geometric layouts within walled enclosures, with pools, fountains and a crossing pattern of canals. Among the most famous of the Mughal gardens existing today are the Taj Mahal in Agra and the Red Fort in Delhi.

Despite India's diverse influences and numerous colonisations, Indian garden design, like Indian culture, has managed to maintain a sense of continuity, and the common architectural motif throughout India's history—the mandala—has remained at the heart of Indian architecture and design. One of the main reasons for this may also be attributed to India's spiritual continuity.

India is a joyous country where religion and its accompanying mythology—most predominantly Hindu, as well as Muslim, Buddhist and Christian—is inextricably linked to all aspects of cultural practice, including design. Plants and decorative elements such as water features and figurines often have symbolic meanings for their placement in a garden: for example, water is seen as the giver of life; the native lotus flower (*Nelumbo nucifera*) as a symbol of divinity, fertility, wealth, knowledge and enlightenment; and statues of the Hindu Lord Ganesh as a symbol of good luck.

Colour also plays a symbolic and significant role in Indian culture and design and is especially evident in fabric and textiles. Home to over 300 indigenous dye plants, India produces the largest variety of textiles in the world and is renowned for its superior craftsmanship—not only for dyed, block-printed, quilted, embroidered and mirror-clad textiles—but also in metalwork, jewellery, marble and pottery.

inspired design ideas

COLOUR

The streets of India are awash with striking, vibrant colour—from bright fabrics to flowers, statues and buildings. An integral part of Indian culture for over 3000 years, colour is symbolic and decorative and plays an important role in all aspects of design.

MARIGOLDS

Both in gardens and in garlands, marigolds are popular throughout India. Natural insect repellents, they are widely used to make protective garlands for safe journeys and to keep the evil spirits away from the gods and their offerings. They are a great way of bringing colour to a garden.

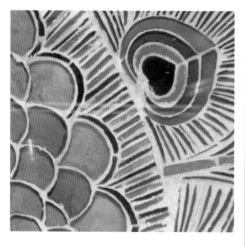

FRAME YOUR VIEW

An integral part of traditional Indian Mughal architecture, the walls of forts, palaces, *havelis* (mansions) and temple compounds often have decorative vantage points from which to catch the breeze and view the streets below, as well as the deserts, mountains, rivers or seas beyond.

PRIVATE SANCTUARY

The Indian garden—both ancient and contemporary—is all about creating your own private sanctuary; a place to relax and unwind, to enjoy family, to escape the heat and to soak up the rays and the rains.

MARBLE

One of the popular natural materials and handicrafts of India, marble—in sculptures, fountains, wall panelling and furniture—is great for the garden, not only for its elegant, pearl-like appearance, but also for its hard-wearing properties. It is also popular for its cooling effect in hot weather.

india at home

The owners of this garden like colour and formal style and wanted a space where they could entertain family and friends. With a high back wall to block freeway noise and little in the way of plants—even grass—this tight space was always going to be a design challenge.

My solution was to draw inspiration from the palace courtyards of India—with their high walls, formal fountains and arched windows—to create a courtyard garden where the walls would add to the design rather than detract from it.

One of the architectural features that impressed me the most in India were the decorative Mughal-style arches; the tough thing, from a design perspective, was how I could replicate these in an Australian backyard. After considering the high cost of importing replica stone arches, I decided to create life-size templates from images I'd taken on my trip. These templates were laid over 12mm fibre-cement sheeting, cut out with a diamond blade and attached to the painted wall, creating stunning arched silhouettes. I then placed a range of timber architraves—limewashed in aqua to suggest the vibrant colours of India—around the arches to frame them like pictures and emphasise the vertical element of the garden.

Between the arches I attached a traditional Indian screen and decorative Mughal-style bowls, potted with bright pink bougainvilleas (*Bougainvillea*). The vibrant ochre colour of the wall and pink of the bougainvillea are complemented by the garden below, with its central feature planting of a pink frangipani (*Plumeria acutifolia* cv)—because the owners' daughter loves frangipanis and their house is full of them—flanked by lilly pillies (*Syzygium leuhmannii*), joy weed (*Alternanthera dentata*) and golden pigeon berry (*Duranta erecta* 'Sheena's Gold').

The pond in front of the wall—featuring a white marble bowl and fountain, traditional Mughal-style spouts and a planting of water lilies (*Nymphaea*)—makes a stunning focal point.

To enhance the courtyard feel, and create privacy for the dining area on one side of the garden and the daybed on the other, we built two feature screen walls with a space between them for access to the garden beyond. Inlaid with traditional Indian grilled windows called Jali screens, the bagged walls also work to create interest by framing the view of the garden from the interior of the home.

Behind the right wall, the dining room features a roof of Natureed to filter the sun and a hard-wearing floor of concrete pavers in the warm ochre colours of Gujarat and the Rajasthani desert. Behind the left wall, the suspended timber daybed is surrounded by a summery planting of crepe myrtle (*Lagerstroemia indica*), native ginger (*Alpinia coerulea* 'Atherton form'), cardamom (*Elletaria cardamomum*) and Chinese fringe flower (*Loropetalum chinense*), and decorated with vibrant Indian fabrics, hanging lamps, ornate cushions and beaded hangings. This Indian sanctuary is now both functional and relaxing.

HANGING DAYBED—
REFER TO SECTION AA

4 X STEPPERS THROUGH
GARDEN TO ACCESS
DAYBED

1100

700

1600

1
CPO1

2
CPO1

1397.1

FOUR OLD STONE
U-SHAPED PLANTERS FROM
POTS ONLINE. POTS
PLANTED WITH 4 x CHILLI
PLANTS AND 4 x MINT

3500

1300

Note: Plans may vary from design to construction

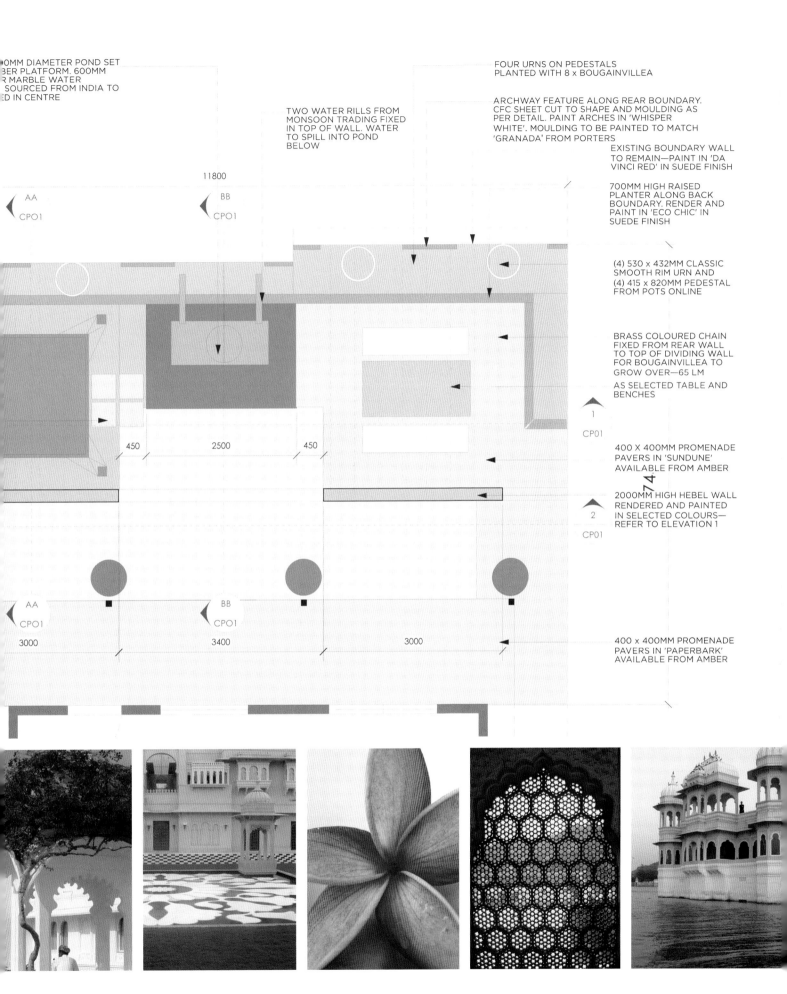

...0MM DIAMETER POND SET
...BER PLATFORM. 600MM
...R MARBLE WATER
... SOURCED FROM INDIA TO
...D IN CENTRE

FOUR URNS ON PEDESTALS
PLANTED WITH 8 x BOUGAINVILLEA

TWO WATER RILLS FROM
MONSOON TRADING FIXED
IN TOP OF WALL. WATER
TO SPILL INTO POND
BELOW

ARCHWAY FEATURE ALONG REAR BOUNDARY.
CFC SHEET CUT TO SHAPE AND MOULDING AS
PER DETAIL. PAINT ARCHES IN 'WHISPER
WHITE'. MOULDING TO BE PAINTED TO MATCH
'GRANADA' FROM PORTERS

EXISTING BOUNDARY WALL
TO REMAIN—PAINT IN 'DA
VINCI RED' IN SUEDE FINISH

700MM HIGH RAISED
PLANTER ALONG BACK
BOUNDARY. RENDER AND
PAINT IN 'ECO CHIC' IN
SUEDE FINISH

11800

AA
CPO1

BB
CPO1

(4) 530 x 432MM CLASSIC
SMOOTH RIM URN AND
(4) 415 x 820MM PEDESTAL
FROM POTS ONLINE

BRASS COLOURED CHAIN
FIXED FROM REAR WALL
TO TOP OF DIVIDING WALL
FOR BOUGAINVILLEA TO
GROW OVER—65 LM

AS SELECTED TABLE AND
BENCHES

1
CP01

450   2500   450

400 X 400MM PROMENADE
PAVERS IN 'SUNDUNE'
AVAILABLE FROM AMBER

2000MM HIGH HEBEL WALL
RENDERED AND PAINTED
IN SELECTED COLOURS—
REFER TO ELEVATION 1

2
CP01

AA
CPO1

BB
CPO1

3000   3400   3000

400 x 400MM PROMENADE
PAVERS IN 'PAPERBARK'
AVAILABLE FROM AMBER

Page 98:

- It's the small decorative touches—stone pots, antique Indian screens, hanging ornaments, hand-painted tins, carvings and religious motifs—that add character and complete this Indian-inspired garden.

The page—clockwise from left:

- Bright pink variegated bougainvillea (*Bougainvillea* cv) was planted in hanging Mughal-style bowls for its vibrant colour and ability to climb and create a growing wall.

- Integral to this Indian-inspired design are the Mughal-style arches created for the rear wall. The centre arch frames an antique *jali* screen and water feature, which uses traditional Indian decorative guttering as water spouts. The pond below is clad in travertine marble and filled with water lilies (*Nympaea*). In the centre an authentic Indian marble bowl fills with water and spills over into the pond water beneath. Marble vases frame each corner of the feature.

- The roof of the dining area is made from Natureed, which is hung between the screening wall and back wall, providing filter from the sun and helping to define the space. The simple timber table and hard-wearing terracotta-coloured concrete pavers echo the warm tones of Gujurat and the Rajasthani desert.

Clockwise from left:

- The timber platform of the daybed is suspended by chains from a pergola structure and clad with an aged timber relief of the Hindu god Ganesha. Coloured glass lanterns, decorative ornaments and curtains hang from the structure, while bright-coloured embroidered cushions and a quilt-covered mattress make this the ultimate in comfort for outdoor relaxation. The garden bed running alongside the daybed and boundary of the property is planted with small leaved lilly pilly (*Syzgium leuhmannii*) to soften the wall, while the smaller plants, ruby joy weed (*Alternanthera dentata* 'Rubiginosa') and golden pigeon berry (*Duranta erecta* 'Sheena's Gold') will eventually grow to form a hedge.

- Beside the daybed we planted cardamom (*Elettaria cardamomum*)—a spice often used in Indian cooking. Closer to the house we planted spearmint (*Mentha spicata*) and coriander (*Coriandrum sativum*) in pots.

design key

Create your own Indian-style outdoor living space by incorporating some of the ideas we came up with for our garden. Introducing specific areas for cooking and dining as well as for relaxation will increase the usability of your garden, as well as the amount of time you spend in it.

PLANTS

TREES
- *Duranta* 'Geisha Girl' GEISHA GIRL PIGEON BERRY
- *Lagerstroemia indica* CREPE MYRTLE
- *Plumeria acutifolia* cv PINK FRANGIPANI
- *Syzgium leuhmannii* SMALL LEAVED LILLY PILLY

SHRUBS
- *Alpinia coerulea* 'Atherton form' NATIVE GINGER
- *Alternanthera dentata* 'Rubiginosa' RUBY JOY WEED
- *Bougainvillea* cv BOUGAINVILLEA (1)
- *Costus comosus* RED TOWER GINGER
- *Duranta erecta* 'Sheena's Gold' SHEENA'S GOLD PIGEON BERRY
- *Elettaria cardamomum* CARDAMOM (3)
- *Gardenia augusta* 'Magnifica' GARDENIA
- *Ixora chinensis* PRINCE OF ORANGE (2)

GROUNDCOVERS
- *Calendula officinalis* POT MARIGOLD
- *Loropetalum chinense* 'China Pink' CHINESE FRINGE FLOWER

WATER PLANTS
- *Nymphaea* WATER LILY

HERBS
- *Coriandrum Sativum* CORIANDER
- *Capsicum annuum* cv CHILLI (4)
- *Mentha spicata* SPEARMINT

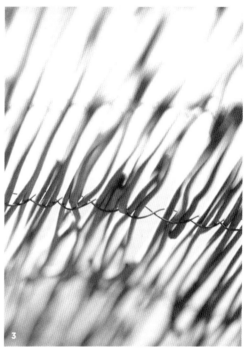

MATERIALS

WALLS
- Bagged screening walls (1) with timber and metal grilled *jali* screens inset as windows (2).
- Rear wall covered with CFC sheeting featuring cut-out Mughal-style arches, painted and decorated with timber beading and Mughal-style hanging planters.

FLOORS
- Terracotta-coloured concrete pavers used both for the floor of the the dining area and the steppers leading from the dining area to the swinging daybed.

OVERHEAD
- Suspended Natureed roof hangs over the dining areas for shade (3).

FEATURES
- Built-in planters—made from timber sleepers covered with CFC sheeting and topped with travertine blocks—run the length of the rear wall.
- Travertine blocks surrounding fibreglass water feature with Mughal-style stone spouts (5) jutting out from the rear planter walls and feature marble bowl and fountain.
- Hanging ornate platform (4) suspended from timber frame and decorated with curtains, hanging lamps. mattress and soft furnishings to create a daybed.

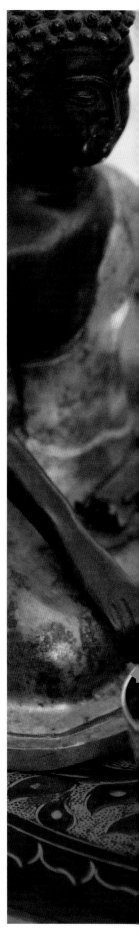

FURNITURE
AND ACCESSORIES

1 & 2 Bright-coloured embroided Indian cushions
and quilt add character and comfort to the
carved wooden daybed.

3 & 5 Hand-painted Indian tins filled with incense
and nuts and a silver teapot with matching cups
and saucers sit atop a carved tray, adding
decorative appeal, practicality and an authentic
aura to the table setting.

4 Colourful sheer curtains, ornate lamps and
beaded accessories hang from the frame of the
daybed—creating an intimate, relaxing and
romantic setting day or night.

6 Marble vases perfectly complement the
travertine and marble water feature in the centre
of the garden. They also provide a place to
display fresh-cut blooms from the garden.

7 A weathered Indian timber and metal screen
hangs as a decorative feature within the centre
arch on the rear wall. A flower garland completes
the traditional feel.

JAMIE BROUGHT HOME:

- Two hand-carved white marble water bowls

Look out for similar Indian and Indian-inspired items at markets and stores in your area.

an english cottage garden

Occupying approximately two-thirds of the island of Great Britain, England is bordered by Scotland to the north, Wales to the west and elsewhere surrounded by sea and the English Channel.

Much of its land is characterised by undulating hills, although a chain of low mountains in the north, known as the Pennines, divides the east and west. The climate is temperate, with ample rainfall all year round, variable seasonal temperatures and sometimes snow in winter or early spring.

History and tradition practically oozes from England's ancient soil. Centuries of invading armies and its close proximity to the European continent have helped shape its history and culture, but England is perhaps recognised more for its historical strength and dominance on the world stage. Pioneers of the Industrial Revolution and once one of the largest empires in history, the influence of English tradition and culture is far-reaching, with a legacy that, even today, extends to almost every corner of the globe.

The evolution of landscape design in England closely mirrors its cultural history. Somehow managing to embrace both formal and informal design, England's landscaping has changed dramatically over the years—in fact for a long time there was no defined 'English style'. Instead, their gardens were influenced by the French or Dutch—symmetrical, geometric and formal—with knot gardens and mazes being two of the most popular features.

By the 18th century, however, a new, naturalistic landscape movement began to flourish alongside the formal look of knot gardens and mazes, incorporating more natural features. Shunning the straight lines of earlier styles, this new direction embraced 'working with nature' and was characterised by wide, undulating green lawns with clumps of trees planted to allow for a natural scene while also conveniently framing interest points. Meticulously planned to give a completely unplanned and informal look, the designs worked on simple, harmonious patterns without obvious symmetry.

As this new desire for informal design took hold, the evolution of the cottage-style garden began. Previously considered peasants' gardens, the original cottage garden was more practical, providing food, herbs and fruit trees, with flowers planted in for an aesthetic touch as well as companion planting purposes. The idea was to plant as closely as possible to reduce the amount of weeding and watering required. With this surge in naturalistic-style planting, the rambling approach and romantic charm of the cottage garden offered a relief from the form and structure of years gone by. In fact, I remember learning in my college days that Australia's own Edna Walling, who is well known for her cottage garden style, used to throw potatoes over her shoulder to find naturalistic planting positions for her flowers. As it grew more popular, the cottage garden became less practical and more decorative, with mass plantings of colour and annuals, plants tumbling from vine-covered arbours and a defining picket fence all typical of this style.

One of the things I love most about English gardens is that there is so much symbology—the knots represent unity and strength, mazes represent 'losing and finding oneself' and the natural form of the cottage garden is all about communing closely with nature. Whether it's formal or informal, or a mixture of the two, there is something to ponder, and that makes the whole experience even better.

inspired design ideas

MAZE

Mazes are a clever way to lend a playful, creative feel to any garden. Not just for kids, mazes offer visual interest in the garden and an opportunity to wander slowly and participate in nature.

ARBOUR

Vine-covered arbours and walkways are essential ingredients in a classic English garden. Their structure is perfect for vines and climbing plants, creating shade and a wonderful, vertical garden. Even without climbing plants, arbours create a theatrical effect.

WHITEWASH

Whitewashed walls are reminiscent of the English cottage style. They can create a dramatic backdrop for rambling roses and creepers and will also reflect light into the darkest corners of any courtyard.

KNOT GARDEN

Traditionally symbolic, knots represent unity, strength and marriage. A knot garden is basically a formal design in a square frame and grown—using a variety of compact hedging plants, aromatic plants and culinary herbs—in such a way that plants weave over and under one another, giving the illusion of a knot. It adds a distinguishing sense of maturity and establishment to your garden.

PICKET FENCE

The picket fence was originally designed for practical purposes, with points to allow the snow to easily fall off. In a modern garden, though, it offers security and provides definition, enhancing the garden's decorative order.

england at home

The owners of this home have young children, so I wanted to create a safe outdoor area that was simultaneously a playful environment for the kids and a restful space for the parents and their friends and family.

A maze was the perfect feature to create a talking point and bring a bit of fun into the garden. We built this one using lauristinus (*Viburnum tinus*) and then added a small, green-growing feature wall of topiaried box hedge (*Buxus microphylla* var. microphylla), trimmed into cones to give a playful feel. Because of water restrictions and a lack of sunlight, we brought in artificial turf with nice long leaf blades to create softness. With this in place, the kids could run through the maze easily and—even better—there's no mowing or watering required of mum and dad!

To create more visual interest and a sense of old-world English charm, I designed a knot garden, again using box hedge (*Buxus microphylla* var. microphylla). This is a traditional decorative technique where hedges are grown to overlap each other and make a 'knot' effect. It takes many years to grow a mature knot garden so we had to be creative in installing this one. To achieve the look, we trimmed one line of box hedging to half height and encouraged the other crossing hedge to grow at full height—this gives the illusion that one overlaps the other.

To screen off the side of the garage, we planted wisteria (*Wisteria sinensis*) in two giant planter boxes and trained it on to lattice. This became an instant green wall and created an intimate outdoor dining or breakfast area looking out over the knot garden.

Down the central spine of the garden we built a series of five arbours and planted climbing roses (*Rosa* 'Iceberg') to grow up and over the top of each structure. In true cottage garden style we then interplanted the arbours with birch trees (*Betula pendula*), ornamental pears (*Pyrus calleryana*) and crepe myrtles (*Lagerstoemia indica*). As an overhead structure they will offer protection and shade the central pathway while also defining each side of the garden. The view from the house is now a stunning tunnel of white beams decorated with tumbling green foliage and flowers. For each successive arbour we dropped the height by 50mm, so that the furthest arbour from the house was lower in height than the one closest to the house. This created an optical illusion of the path being longer than it really is and gave visual depth to the garden.

Built-in bench seating made out of whitewashed timber allowed for much-needed storage space in the entertaining area. Then, to maximise the potential for outdoor living and create a place for gatherings, we covered the dining area with a clear corrugated roofing that would allow the sun in but not the rain.

As a final touch—to provide an element of safety and to give definition—we enclosed the garden with a decorative, white picket fence and added greenery with a surrounding European hedge of zelkova (*Zelkova serrata*). We then espaliered a quince tree (*Chaenomeles speciosa*) against it to soften it.

19 x *Lavandula angustfolia* —
'Hidcote'

5 x *Michelia* 'Scented Pearl'

2 x *Anenome* x *hybrida*

SYNTHETIC TURF TO SECRE
GARDEN

TIMBER GARDEN EDGE (12 L

2 x *Anenome* x *hybrida*

PICKET FENCE AND GATE

8 x *Gardenia jasminoides* 'R

7 x *Trachelospermum* —
jasminoides 'Tricolor'

12 x *Agapanthus* 'Peter Pan'

6 x *Lavandula angustfolia* 'H

15 x *Convolvulus cneorum*

RENDERED BLOCK WALLS
IN SELECTED COLOUR

40 x *Buxus microphylla* (14C

NEW RAMP TO BE CUT
INTO GARDEN
20 x *Sedum* 'Autumn Joy'
30 x *Buxus microphylla* (20
NEW SANDSTONE PAVING
RAMP AND PATH

12 x *Agapanthus* 'Peter Pan'
Existing *Convolvulus* —

TIMBER BENCH SEATS
3600 X 500 X450H MM

EXISTING SANDSTONE PAV
TO REMAIN

12 x *Agapanthus* 'Peter Pan'

PERGOLA WITH PERSPEX R
SHEETING OVER TOP

12 x *Gardenia jasminoides*
'Radicans'

LANDSCAPE PLA
1 Scale: 1:50

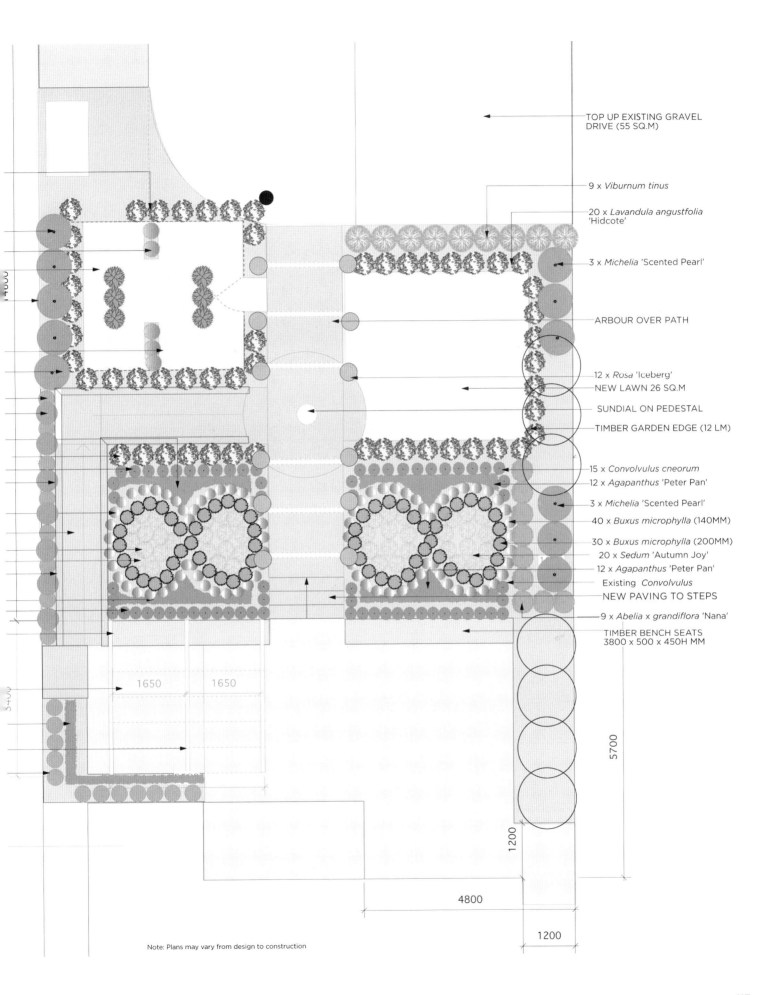

TOP UP EXISTING GRAVEL
DRIVE (55 SQ.M)

9 x *Viburnum tinus*

20 x *Lavandula angustfolia*
'Hidcote'

3 x *Michelia* 'Scented Pearl'

ARBOUR OVER PATH

12 x *Rosa* 'Iceberg'
NEW LAWN 26 SQ.M

SUNDIAL ON PEDESTAL

TIMBER GARDEN EDGE (12 LM)

15 x *Convolvulus cneorum*
12 x *Agapanthus* 'Peter Pan'

3 x *Michelia* 'Scented Pearl'

40 x *Buxus microphylla* (140MM)

30 x *Buxus microphylla* (200MM)
20 x *Sedum* 'Autumn Joy'
12 x *Agapanthus* 'Peter Pan'

Existing *Convolvulus*
NEW PAVING TO STEPS

9 x *Abelia* x *grandiflora* 'Nana'

TIMBER BENCH SEATS
3800 x 500 x 450H MM

1650   1650

5700

1200

4800

1200

Note: Plans may vary from design to construction

Previous page:

- Hidden behind its own picket fence, this 'secret garden' with its maze and topiaried box hedge (*Buxus microphylla* var. microphylla) trimmed into cones brings a playful element to the garden, adding a sense of fun and adventure for the kids.

- Sheer lengths of white fabric line the ceiling of the pergola, softening the structure and diffusing the sunlight. Antique birdcages double as hanging planters for pink and white cyclamen (*Cyclamen persicum*), adding colour to the entertaining area.

This page, clockwise from left:

- This brightly striped fabric panel provides a screen for the garage as well as a colourful backdrop for the children's maze.

- A traditional wrought-iron outdoor dining setting makes a cosy retreat in a quiet corner of the garden.

- Distressed wrought-iron motifs decorate the fence between plantings of camellias (*Camellia sasanqua*) espaliered on to lattice panels.

Facing page:

- In the centre of the garden a series of five arbours, built at slightly different heights, add visual depth and definition to the garden. Climbing roses (*Rosa* 'Iceberg') will grow to provide overhead shade. A simple timber bench seat with colourful cushions provides a focal point at the end of the path.

design key

Create your own English-style outdoor living space by incorporating some of the ideas we came up with for our garden. Existing structures may present opportunities for design—a blank wall might be perfect for creating a colourful feature or for mounting decorations.

PLANTS

TREES
- *Betula pendula* SILVER BIRCH
- *Camellia sasanqua* SASANQUA CAMELLIA (4)
- *Lagerstroemia indica* CREPE MYRTLE
- *Magnolia grandiflora* 'Little Gem' LITTLE GEM MAGNOLIA
- *Michelia* 'Scented Pearl' SCENTED PEARL MICHELIA
- *Pyrus calleryana* ORNAMENTAL PEAR
- *Zelkova serrata* JAPANESE ZELKOVA

SHRUBS
- *Buxus microphylla* var. microphylla KOREAN BOX (3)
- *Chaenomeles speciosa* FLOWERING QUINCE
- *Escallonia* 'Pink Pixie' PINK PIXIE ESCALLONIA
- *Gardenia jasminoides* 'Radicans' CREEPING GARDENIA
- *Lavandula angustifolia* 'Hidcote' HIDCOTE LAVENDER
- *Viburnum tinus* LAURISTINUS

GROUNDCOVERS AND CLIMBERS
- *Abelia* x *grandiflora* 'Nana' DWARF ABELIA
- *Agapanthus* 'Peter Pan' PETER PAN AGAPANTHUS
- *Anemone* x *hybrida* JAPANESE WIND FLOWER
- *Convolvulus cneorum* SILVERBUSH
- *Cyclamen persicum* CYCLAMEN (2)
- *Hebe* 'Emerald Green' EMERALD GREEN HEBE (3)
- *Rosa* 'Iceberg' CLIMBING ICEBERG ROSE
- *Sedum* 'Autumn Joy' AUTUMN JOY STONECROP (1, 3)
- *Trachelospermum jasminoides* 'Tricolor' VARIEGATED STAR JASMINE
- *Wisteria sinensis* WISTERIA

MATERIALS

WALLS
- Traditional timber picket fencing with gate painted in white limewash (1).
- Brightly coloured fabric fixed to the wall screens the garage and adds a playful touch (2).
- Lattice panels fixed to the fence allow plants to climb up and through them (3).
- Brick edging and retaining walls define pathways (1) and separate the entertaining area and garden.

FLOORS
- Sandstone pavers were used to match the existing paved areas. Pale in colour, they tone with the whitewash surrounds and allow the colours of the cottage garden to stand out.
- Artificial turf was laid in the maze as a low-maintenance flooring option and to help overcome the challenge of a heavily shaded area.

OVERHEAD
- Timber arbours, each built 50mm smaller than the previous one, painted white.
- Timber pergola with clear Perspex roof to allow for year-round use (3).

FEATURES
- Built-in seating made from hardwood timber lines the front of the retaining wall.

FURNITURE AND ACCESSORIES

1 Candles create atmosphere for any outdoor occasion. Placed in these simple silver holders they add an elegant touch to the table setting.

2 Painted timber rabbits and colourful windmills placed in the maze add a playful touch to the garden and are fun for the children to discover.

3 Table accessories such as this angel-winged *objet d'art* tone with the white-washed surrounds and are a small but effective way to help set the mood.

4 A traditional element of English garden design, this sundial has been placed on a post in the corner of the knot garden for an authentic touch.

5 & 6 The brightly striped change-rooms that line England's Brighton beach inspired these stripey cushions and deck chairs. Adding both colour and comfort, the different coloured patterns reflect the intended informal 'thrown together' look of a typical English cottage garden. An old birdbath has been recycled and transformed to make an interesting side table. The white-washed timber arbour is a central feature defining each side of the garden and allows for overhead shade in the summer months.

7 Distressed wrought-iron motifs decorate the fence boundary and add a sense of antiquity.

JAMIE BROUGHT HOME:

- Sundial
- White birdcages from the Columbia Road flower markets

Look out for similar English and English-inspired items at markets and stores in your area.

a mexican courtyard

mexico is a hot land of bright colours, private thriving courtyards, eye-catching collectables and drought-loving plants. When it comes to garden design, Mexico is an inspiration.

Home to around 26,000 species of plants, it is one of the richest horticultural regions on Earth, ranging from desert cactuses and succulents in the north, to pine forests, jungle and tropical palms in the south. Within a land of extremes, Mexican living is—by choice as well as necessity—focused on the outdoors.

Places to catch the breeze in summer and the sun in winter, as well as to escape the chaos of the urban environment, gardens are important to Mexican culture. At the heart of this is the Mexican architectural tradition of placing living areas around internal walled courtyards, leaving little distinction between inside and out. Private and reflective, these outdoor rooms are designed to be 'lived in'—spaces for reclining, dining, contemplation and celebration.

Historically, both the Aztec and Spanish traditions have influenced this style of living and building. All Mexican towns were built around a central plaza or park, complete with gardens and public fountains from which people and animals would draw water. With the arrival of the Spanish came the advent of the most distinctive of Mexican architectural features—the wall. Derived directly from the Hispano-Moorish tradition in Spain at the time of the conquest and for reasons of protection and security, high, thick walls—made from adobe, or stone, brick or wood often rendered in clay or cement—were built around Mexican homes. The interior courtyards they created became private garden oases, complete with fountains, plants, colour and collectables.

Remaining as a divider between public and private space, these walls and their private central courtyards became an integral part of Mexican architectural design. Contemporary designers Luis Barragan and Ricardo Legorreta famously continued this style, incorporating other Mexican traditions of bold colour and fountains into their designs. My visits to Barragan's home and studio were simply a dream, and his courage with colour and architecture constantly inspires me.

Like walls and fountains, the colours of Mexico are also steeped in culture and history. Ancient monuments, tombs and ruins have been found with vivid painted exteriors and frescoes displaying the same vibrant colours—deep reds and pinks, ochre yellows and turquoise blues—of the boldly painted village walls, shops and homes seen throughout modern history. Integral to cultural beliefs of chance, destiny, luck and good fortune, these colours are derived from nature, festivals, celebrations and ceremonial tradition, and have become synonymous worldwide with Mexican culture.

These influences of bold colour and geometric patterns were also integrated into Mexican arts, crafts and textiles, including the fabulous woven rugs and pottery still made today.

inspired design ideas

BOLD-COLOURED WALLS

The most distinctive of Mexican architectural features, bold-coloured walls provide both an aesthetic and practical function—creating a division between public and private space and a stunning backdrop for the gardens within.

THE MEXICAN COURTYARD

Tucked behind high, private walls, the interior courtyards of the traditional Mexican home are secluded family oases—a natural retreat from the severe urban environment, as well as a space to entertain and escape the harsh climate.

TEXTILES

Mexico is renowned for its fabulous array of woven rugs and textiles. The bold red, orange and yellow shades are derived from cochineal, the traditional dye of pre-Hispanic Mexico, which is made from the native cochineal bug that lives on the pads of the nopal cactus (*Opuntia*).

DROUGHT-HARDY PLANTS

Mexico's native cactuses and succulents are some of the most drought-tolerant species in the world. Storing water within their trunks and bulbous leaves, many also have a barrier of spikes to protect their stores from animals.

BLACK POTTERY

The black pottery famous to the Oaxaca area of Mexico is simply stunning. It only comes from this part of the world and gets its appearance from the clay, which has metals in it that oxidise during the firing process.

mexico at home

The owners of this garden love colour, spending time at the beach and entertaining frequently for family and friends. Living by the coast, where water restrictions are a concern, they wanted a drought-hardy garden.

Taking design inspiration from their lifestyle, as well as from the location and style of their home, which featured a stucco-style render and chimney above the existing barbecue area, I looked to the courtyard gardens of Mexico for further inspiration.

Mexican design is all about colour, and I wanted to use vibrant shades to create an exciting and stimulating environment for the owners and their young children to entertain and play in. Working with a bold palette of sunburnt orange, Frida Kahlo blue—inspired by my visit to her home—and vivid pink, the design focus was to create a large, functional entertaining area-cum-comfortable outdoor living room with a casual, beachside feel.

To achieve this, we introduced a large feature wall with built-in bench seating and screening to define the space, and improved the cooking area by adding a new barbecue with additional bench space for food preparation and cooking utensils. The wall, bench seating and chimney were all rendered and painted in the Mexican style, with the old chimney now resembling the customary Mexican chiminea. The wall featured traditional recessed shelves to display *objets d'art*, in which we placed the stunning black pottery I sourced from the Oaxaca region of Mexico.

Recycled timber was used to frame the feature wall and build the frames of the screens. The screens themselves were made from suspended sheets of Perspex digitally printed with a pattern scanned from a rug I also sourced from Mexico—which is also placed within the garden atop the table as a runner. Both decorative and functional, these screens not only enhance the intimacy of the outdoor living space, but also provide privacy from neighbouring properties and a great view from within the home.

Timber sleepers with pebbles in between were used to create the floor beneath the screens, introducing a beach-style element to the design. The inclusion of the rendered daybed, complete with Aztec-inspired raised headrest, enhances the relaxed beachside feel, as does the coastal-inspired planting scheme.

Bold, architectural and drought-hardy, the plant selection captures the very essence of Mexico—from the giant yuccas (*Yucca elephantipes*), to the Mexican lilies (*Beschorneria yuccoides*), to the striking foliage of the agaves (*Agave desmettiana* 'Variegata' and *Agave attenuata*), to the wonderful colours of the pig face (*Mesembryanthemum*), marigolds (*Tagetes*) and flapjacks (*Kalanchoe luciae*). With a focus on texture, form and durability, many of the plants selected are Mexican natives, known for their low water requirements and reliability in the Australian climate. They provide a stunning contrast to the vibrant colour palette.

RETAIN EXISTING PLANTING AND
SUPPLEMENT WITH RELOCATED PLANTS

1 x *Aloe bainsii*

PROPOSED 1800 X 600 X 400MM
PINK RENDERED DAYBED

4 x *Metrosideros excelsa*

3 x *Yucca sp.* to 1.5M
11 x *Agave 'El Mirador's Gold'*
RECYCLED HARDWOOD TIMBER
FRAME WITH 3 PERSPEX PRINTS SEE
SECTION B-B

REUSE EXISTING SANDSTONE BLOCKS
SET IN 40 x *Teucrium fruticans*

23 x *Kalanchoe 'Flap Jacks'*

MATURE CACTUS SPIKES TO 2M

RETAIN EXISTING *Meterosideros Sp.*

RELOCATE EXISTING TRAMPOLINE

FOLD OUT CLOTHESLINE

REAR OF FEATURE WALL TO BE
PAINTED ORANGE

EXISTING GATES TO BE PAINTED
HIGH GLOSS BLUE

Note: Plans may vary from design to construction

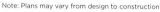

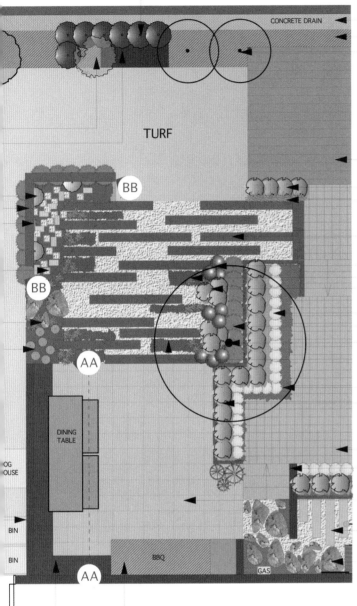

TURF

BB

BB

AA

DINING TABLE

OG OUSE

BIN

BIN

BBQ

GAS

AA

CONCRETE DRAIN

7 x *Yucca 'Jewel'*

CONCRETE DRAINAGE CHANNEL

RETAIN EXISTING PLANTING

RETAIN EXISTING GOLDEN CANE PALMS

EXISTING DECK WITH ROOF OVER

4 x *Beschorneria yuccoides*
9 x *Crassula ovata*

RECYCLED HARDWOOD SLEEPERS IN GOLD DECO GRANITE

9 x *Crassula ovata*
9 x *Kalanchoe 'Flap Jacks'*
6 x *Beschornaria yuccoides*

60 x *Tagetes sp.*
7 x *Agave 'El Mirador's Gold'*

RETAIN EXISTING *Delonix regia*

40 x *Senecio serpens*

72 x *Lampranthus aurantiacus* @ 25M2

13 x *Beschorneria yuccoides* UNDERPLANTED WITH 30 x *Sedum morganianum* TO TRAIL OVER RETAINING WALL

EXISTING TERRACOTTA COLOURED PAVING

RENDERED BESSER BLOCK WALL TO TOP OF LANDING

400 x 400MM HIMALAYAN SANDSTONE PAVERS FROM AMBER

EXISTING OUTDOOR SHOWER. RE-USE EXISTING SANDSTONE BLOCKS TO CREATE RAISED GRILL

IRREGULAR SHAPED SANDSTONE SLABS IN GRAVEL WITH 25 x *Lampranthus aurantiacus* @ 25M2

EXISTING BRICK BBQ AND CHIMNEY. RENDERED AND PAINTED TO LOOK LIKE ADOBE

RENDERED 200MM THICK ADOBE STYLE FEATURE WALL AND BENCH SEAT. SEE SECTION A-A

Page 132—from top:

- This rustic blue chair was nearly thrown away until we discovered it and found it the ideal garden corner.

- Succulents such as agaves (*Agave attenuata* and *Agave desmettiana* 'Variegata'), flapjacks (*Kalanchoe luciae*) and blue chalk sticks (*Senecio serpens*) are all typical plants you might find in a Mexican-inspired garden.

This page—clockwise from bottom left:

- These tall peruvian apple cactuses (*Cereus peruvianus*) add verticality and interest to the planting scheme, while the brightly coloured pig face (*Mesembryanthemum* hybrid) planted at their feet softens the effect, adding colour and contrast.

- Timber sleepers of varying lengths surrounded by white crushed quartz pebbles introduce a relaxed, beach-style element to the design.

- Mexican natives thrive in the Australian climate and are perfect for this garden design.

Facing page:

- The natural-style groundcover and architectural plantings surrounding the entertaining area connect the space with nature and create a dramatic effect against the bright-coloured walls.

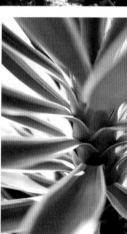

Facing page:

- Mexican design is all about colour. This vivid Frida Kahlo-inspired blue wall features inset shelving painted brilliant pink. The traditional Mexican black pottery placed in these shelves creates a dramatic and bold effect against the vibrant colour. Beneath the shelves the built-in bench seating is made comfortable by Aztec-inspired soft furnishings.

This page—clockwise from left:

- Recycled timber sleepers were used to build up a garden bed and create a planter wall filled with a mix of succulents and drought-hardy plants. Planted in repitition, the Mexican lilies (*Beschorneria yuccoides*) within the bed and the agaves (*Agave desmettiana* 'Variegata') beneath create a stunning effect.

- The functionality of the outdoor cooking and entertaining area was enhanced by installing a new barbecue and extending the bench for food and drink preparation. Long timber tables and bench seating maximises movement around the space, as well as the number of diners possible.

design key

Create your own Mexican-style outdoor living space by incorporating some of the planting, material, furniture and accessories ideas we came up with for our garden. It's amazing how easy it is to get a Mexican look just by adding a few key design elements.

PLANTS

TREES AND CACTUSES
- *Yucca elephantipes* GIANT YUCCA
- *Cereus peruvianus* PERUVIAN APPLE (2)

SHRUBS
- *Agave attenuata* AGAVE
- *Agave desmettiana* 'Variegata' VARIEGATED SMOOTH AGAVE (3)
- *Beschorneria yuccoides* MEXICAN LILY
- *Kalanchoe luciae* FLAPJACKS (1)
- *Metrosideros excelsa* NEW ZEALAND CHRISTMAS BUSH
- *Teucrium fruticans* BUSH GERMANDER
- *Yucca elephantipes* 'Jewel' JEWEL YUCCA

GROUNDCOVERS
- *Crassula ovata* 'Gollum' GOLLUM JADE PLANT
- *Mesembryanthemum* hybrid PIG FACE (4)
- *Sedum morganianum* DONKEYS TAILS
- *Senecio rowleyanus* STRING OF BEADS
- *Senecio serpens* BLUE CHALK STICKS
- *Tagetes* hybrid MARIGOLDS
- *Tillandsia usneoides* SPANISH MOSS

MATERIALS

WALLS
- Rendered adobe-style feature wall with cut-in display shelves (4), decorative grilled window (2), built-in bench seating.
- Recycled hardwood timber frames with suspended Perspex privacy screens.

FLOORS
- Sandstone paved floor for the cooking and dining area.
- Timber sleepers surrounded by white crushed quartz pebbles (5) connect the paved and screened areas. The crushed quartz pebbles extend into the natural-style garden (1).

FEATURES
- Built-in rendered cooking area with barbecue, chiminea-style chimney and preparation benches.
- Rendered daybed with inclined headrest.
- Planter wall of recycled timber sleepers (3).

FURNITURE AND ACCESSORIES

1 The built-in daybed has an Aztec-inspired raised headrest and made-to-measure foam mattress. Scatter cushions add colour and comfort.

2 Sourced direct from Mexico, this traditional Mexican rug was used to create the decorative pattern for the hanging Perspex screens. It is also used as a table runner, adding an authentic look and feel while also softening the setting.

3 When decorating your garden, look around to see if you can recycle any old bits and pieces. We salvaged this discarded blue chair and found that it fitted in perfectly with the overall theme.

4 Mexican black pottery, also sourced from my travels, introduces character and help set the tone to this Mexico-inspired theme. In some of these we placed candles, which create a warm, inviting glow in the evenings.

5 The wagon wheel, sourced from the family home via the owner's father, provided the perfect rustic touch to the garden.

6 Brightly coloured embroidered cushions add a light-hearted, celebratory feel to the design and combine well with the earthy tones of the weathered leather cushions that are symbolic of the Aztec influence.

JAMIE BROUGHT HOME:

- Traditional Mexican rug
- Black pottery

Look out for similar Mexican and Mexican-inspired items at markets and stores in your area.

a thai retreat

from bustling markets to hushed golden temples, from cool misty mountains to hot chaotic cities, from fiery chilli to sweet jam, all in one mouthful—Thailand is a land of diversity and pleasing contradictions.

Located within the tropics of South East Asia, on the Gulf of Thailand and the Andaman Sea, Thailand boasts a diverse botany of around 15,000 plant species and is home to the largest number of orchid species in Asia. Bright, scented blooms punctuate thick vegetation; mist hangs over green hills symmetrically terraced for rice; and bamboo walls hide jungle foliage, fruit trees and thriving private oases in the centre of international cities. When it comes to gardens, Thailand is brimming with hidden treasures.

A relaxed and reverent culture, every aspect of Thai daily life is influenced by the unifying faith of Buddhism. With some 90 per cent of the population as followers, Buddhist philosophy and symbolic aesthetic flows over into every area of cultural practice, including garden design, architecture, arts and crafts and ornamentation.

Providing areas for prayer and restful retreat, Thai gardens are all about beauty, balance and harmony. Modern gardens tend to emphasise the country's tropical luxuriance, blending native and imported plants in an artful, jungle-inspired way, often with a space for herbs, spices and fruits used in cooking. However, traditional gardens were highly structured and steeped in superstition.

In traditional Thai gardens, plants, flowers, herbs and fruit trees were positioned in specific places around the garden. Plants bearing auspicious names—especially those associated with luck and protection—were given pride of place, while those bearing inauspicious names were taboo. Other common elements of traditional gardens include glazed water jars, fragrance, colour and clipped tree art, called *mai dat*. Many of these elements remain popular today, especially planting fragrant and colourful flowers like jasmine (*Jasminum sambac*), *chuan chom* or desert rose (*Adenium obesum*), angel's wings (*Caladium bicolor*) and crotons (*Codiaeum variegatum*).

All Thai homes also have a house of spirits (*san phra phum*)—a small house commonly situated in the corner of the garden, where the owner of the home places daily offerings to feed the spirits, assuring good blessings. Other common structures in the Thai garden include open pavilions, called sala, often filled with cushions to relax in and take respite from the heat and humidity. These pavilions are usually made of wood, boasting carved decoration and high-pitched roofs representative of traditional Thai home and temple architecture.

Traditional architecture, like the traditional handicrafts of woodcarving and silk-making, display impressive attention to detail and superior craftsmanship. Articles used for practical purposes, like intricately carved teak furniture and eating utensils inlaid with beautiful patterns of mother of pearl, are no exception: the beauty and harmony of Thai culture seeps into every aspect of living.

inspired design ideas

CREATIVE USE OF SPACE

Thai gardens, especially those found on rooftops, balconies and courtyards in the city, might be confined to small spaces, but they are definitely not constricted by size. Using space creatively allows a slice of nature to be brought to any sized outdoor area.

RICE TERRACES

Rice farming is a huge part of Thai culture and forms the base of Thailand's fragrant and flavoursome cuisine. Dominating the visual landscape, the complex symmetry of the rice terrace provides inspired ideas for design.

WOOD CARVING

Thai people are passionate about their handicrafts and carving is one of their specialities. Intricate pieces add a sense of age, character and culture to an outdoor space.

TRADITIONAL ORNAMENTS

Traditional temple-inspired ornaments are important elements in Thai-style gardens. Made from materials such as wood, glass mosaic, gold leaf, porcelain and stone, traditional ornaments include items such as Buddhist statues and spirit houses.

THAI SILK

Handwoven Thai silk is known for its exquisite lustre, thick texture and striking contrast of shimmering colours, including vivid magenta and emerald green, deep red and sapphire blue. Accessories made from Thai silk make stunning additions outdoors.

thailand at home

The owners of this garden wanted a low-fuss, low-maintenance tropical garden with a shaded area to retreat from the often harsh Queensland sun. They also wanted to introduce some colour and greenery to the space.

Starting with a narrow area featuring a rectangular pool surrounded by a colourbond fence and high, glare-reflecting concrete walls at the top, this space did everything it could to deter rather than invite. Drawing inspiration from the tropical climate and the resort-style setting of the pool, I looked to the open pavilions and lush colourful gardens of Thailand for inspiration.

High walls are a feature of city living, and one I like—not just because they provide privacy, but because I see them as a dramatic backdrop to decorate and turn into a feature. When I first saw the walls of this garden, I began to envisage climbers meandering their way across vivid colour, and then I thought, why not go one step further? Why not build a vertical garden to create a cascade of tropical foliage—orchids (*Cymbidium*, *Dendrobium* and *Phalaenopsis*) and jasmine (*Jasminum sambac* and *Mandevilla*)—all the plants that I'd been so inspired by in Thailand but didn't quite have the space for in this confined area.

The structure of the vertical garden provided a framework from which to build a slatted-roof pavilion, creating much-needed shade and an inviting living space to relax in while being surrounded by the cooling effect of nature.

To introduce a more organic, human-friendly horizontal surface that would avoid soaking up too much heat, stop the glare and be much more inviting to walk on barefoot, we installed a wooden deck using a product called Ezydeck,

which is sourced from off-cuts of sustainable, managed forests and features a nylon interlocking substructure. To soften the surface even further, we embedded plants into the deck, avoiding the clutter of pots (another hard-surface element) and achieving a more striking visual outcome with a more direct connection to nature.

The old pool fence was replaced with frameless glass, and the boundary wall was decorated with pillars of carved floral motifs, punctuated with Natureed and a series of foliage—Mother in Law's tongue (*Sansevieria trifasciata* 'Laurentii') for verticality and crotons (*Codiaeum variegatum*) for constant tropical colour. The masonry piers were decorated with four beautiful hand-carved *ngahs* (serpents), the repetitious installation working to increase the visual length of the wall and create the illusion of space.

At the end of the pool we built a raised garden bed of contrasting native grasses from two types of mat rush (*Lomandra* 'Tanika' and *Lomandra* 'Wingarra')—directly inspired by the rice terraces of Thailand. We also surrounded the existing garden beds with ginger (*Zingiber spectabilis* 'Cocoa Delight'), crotons (*Codiaeum variegatum*) and rhoeo (*Tradescantia spathacea* 'Vittata').

Two beautiful potted Mauritius hemp (*Furcraea foetida* 'Mediopicta') were placed in front of a feature wall painted with a green wash to create a chalky, aged effect, and decorated with a hand-carved antique timber architrave. Traditional triangle cushions were placed beneath this to create a daybed and decorated with additional cushions of Thai silk and hand-carved orange candles to evoke the relaxed and spiritual essence of Thai lifestyle and culture.

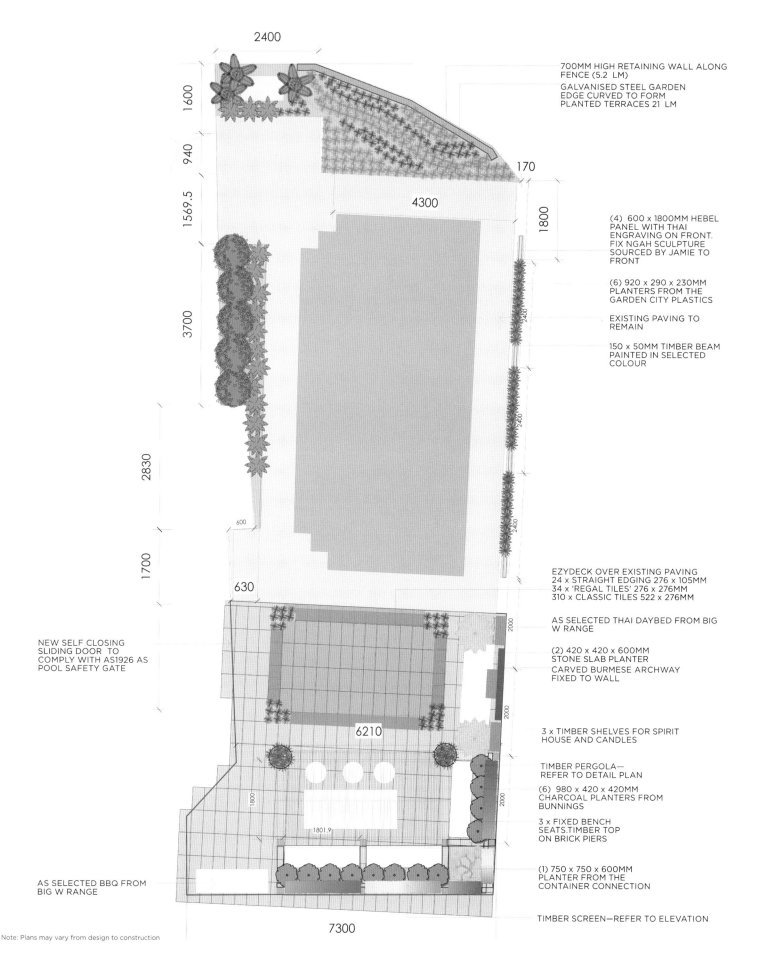

2400

1600

940

1569.5

3700

2830

1700

600

630

2830

170

4300

1800

700MM HIGH RETAINING WALL ALONG
FENCE (5.2 LM)

GALVANISED STEEL GARDEN
EDGE CURVED TO FORM
PLANTED TERRACES 21 LM

(4) 600 x 1800MM HEBEL
PANEL WITH THAI
ENGRAVING ON FRONT.
FIX NGAH SCULPTURE
SOURCED BY JAMIE TO
FRONT

(6) 920 x 290 x 230MM
PLANTERS FROM THE
GARDEN CITY PLASTICS

EXISTING PAVING TO
REMAIN

150 x 50MM TIMBER BEAM
PAINTED IN SELECTED
COLOUR

EZYDECK OVER EXISTING PAVING
24 x STRAIGHT EDGING 276 x 105MM
34 x 'REGAL TILES' 276 x 276MM
310 x CLASSIC TILES 522 x 276MM

AS SELECTED THAI DAYBED FROM BIG
W RANGE

(2) 420 x 420 x 600MM
STONE SLAB PLANTER
CARVED BURMESE ARCHWAY
FIXED TO WALL

3 x TIMBER SHELVES FOR SPIRIT
HOUSE AND CANDLES

TIMBER PERGOLA—
REFER TO DETAIL PLAN

(6) 980 x 420 x 420MM
CHARCOAL PLANTERS FROM
BUNNINGS

3 x FIXED BENCH
SEATS.TIMBER TOP
ON BRICK PIERS

(1) 750 x 750 x 600MM
PLANTER FROM THE
CONTAINER CONNECTION

TIMBER SCREEN—REFER TO ELEVATION

NEW SELF CLOSING
SLIDING DOOR TO
COMPLY WITH AS1926 AS
POOL SAFETY GATE

AS SELECTED BBQ FROM
BIG W RANGE

6210

1800

1801.9

7300

Note: Plans may vary from design to construction

Page 152—clockwise from bottom left:

- Timber decking and pebble-lined tropical plantings introduce a natural, Thai-style feel.

- Creating a vertical garden using wall-mounted timber planters was a clever way to not only soften and mask the high surrounding wall, but to also allow for an abundance of planting we would otherwise not have had the space for.

- Enveloped by a vertical garden, these bench seats are the perfect spot to relax.

- Chilean jasmine (*Mandevilla*) spills from the vertical planters, creating a cascade of sweet smelling colour and foliage.

This page—clockwise from top:

- The timber-squared deck adds interest and softens the horizontal surface. Embedding plants into the deck eliminates the need for pots.

- Authentic hard-carved *ngahs* decorate the panels alongside the pool. They add character and interest to the design.

Facing page:

- An antique hand-carved Thai architrave creates a stunning focal point in the garden. The addition of colourful Thai-style cushions and over-sized religious candles instantly creates a relaxed and peaceful atmosphere in the garden.

Facing page—clockwise from bottom:

- The vertical garden allowed me to be able to plant more of the tropical plants I'd been so inspired by in Thailand. They also allowed the entertaining area to be filled with an abundance of plants.

- Giant birds of paradise (*Strelitzia reginae*) were inserted into the deck to allow a closer connection with nature. Growing directly upwards, their architectual form achieves a striking, dramatic look.

- A series of pots set atop the slatted timber roof of the pergola were planted with the colourful and architectural rhoeo (*Tradescantia spathacea* 'Vittata').

This page, clockwise from left:

- Adding an elegant, artistic touch to the garden, the carvings in the panels alongside the pool replicate the form of Mother in Law's tongue (*Sansevieria trifasciata* 'Laurentii') planted either side of them.

- Typical of any Thai retreat, these traditional triangle cushions add an aura of relaxation and appealing comfort to the garden.

design key

Create your own Thai-style outdoor living space by incorporating some of the planting, material, furniture and accessories ideas we came up with for our garden. You can adapt these ideas to an outdoor area of any size—from a small balcony to a corner of a large garden.

PLANTS

SHRUBS
- *Bambusa eutuldoides* 'China Gold' CHINA GOLD BAMBOO
- *Codiaeum variegatum* CROTON (3)
- *Cymbidium* hybrid CYMBIDIUM ORCHID
- *Furcraea foetida* 'Mediopicta' MAURITIUS HEMP (4)
- *Heliconia* hybrid HELICONIA
- *Plumeria pudica* BRIDAL BOUQUET
- *Sansevieria trifrasciata* 'Laurentii' MOTHER IN LAW'S TONGUE (1)
- *Schefflera arboricola* 'Madam de Smet' VARIEGATED UMBRELLA PLANT
- *Shibatea kumasaca* FORTUNE INVITING BAMBOO
- *Strelitzia reginae* BIRD OF PARADISE
- *Zingiber spectabilis* 'Cocoa Delight' COCOA DELIGHT GINGER

CLIMBERS
- *Mandevilla* cv CHILEAN JASMINE
- *Trachelospermum jasminoides* STAR JASMINE

GROUNDCOVERS AND GRASSES
- *Aptenia cordifolia* BABY SUN ROSE
- *Lomandra* 'Tanika' TANIKA MAT RUSH
- *Lomandra* 'Wingarra' WINGARRA MAT RUSH
- *Lomandra concertifolia* 'Little Con' LITTLE CON MAT RUSH
- *Lomandra concertifolia* 'Little Pal' LITTLE PAL MAT RUSH
- *Tradescantisa spathacea* 'Vittata' VAR. RHOEO (2)

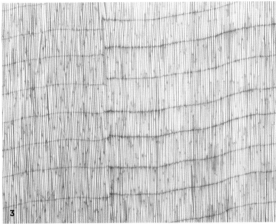

MATERIALS

WALLS
- Built-in timber bench seating and slatted timber planter boxes line the wall of the entertaining area (4).
- Decoratively engraved Hebel panels (5) and Natureed create a feature along the retaining wall surrounding the pool.
- Natureed lines the retaining wall behind the terraced garden (3).
- A frameless glass fence divides the pool and decked entertaining area.

FLOORS
- A timber deck constructed from squares of Ezydeck—which features a nylon interlocking substructure—covers the existing concrete floor (2). Some squares are left free to allow for tropical plantings lined with gravel.

OVERHEAD
- Hardwood timber pergola with slatted roof provides shade for the entertaining area (1).

FEATURES
- A terraced garden constucted with steel edging forms a feature at the far end of the pool.

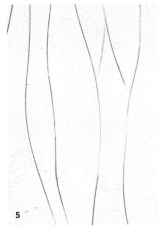

FURNITURE
AND ACCESSORIES

1 & 3 Oversized religious candles in the traditional saffron colour of monks robes invoke a restful, ambient atmosphere while also providing light and warmth. Decorative ball lanterns studded throughout the garden complement the effect.

2 Buddhist-style sculptures add interest and authenticity to the Thai-style theme.

4 The outdoor table setting is kept simple and natural to blend with the timber of the built-in bench seating and surrounds. The Thai silk bench runners add colour and comfort.

5 Sourced direct from Thailand, these hand-carved *ngahs* were placed along the boundary wall surrounding the pool: their aged patina add character and charm to the design.

6 & 7 The placement of ground-level Thai triangle cushions creates a lovely relaxation space; allowing a closer connection to the foliage and a sense of seclusion and intimacy. The Jim Thompson-designed silk cushions add softness and help to set the overall mood.

8 Placed on a feature wall, this intricately hand-carved antique Thai wooden architrave creates a stunning central focal point as it frames and defines the relaxation space.

JAMIE BROUGHT HOME:

■ Antique Thai architraves

■ Carved *ngahs*—sacred serpents to protect Buddha

■ Religious candles

■ Triangular cushions

■ Thai silk

Look out for similar Thai and Thai-inspired items at markets and stores in your area.

an italian villa

family and friends gathered around a long table laden with fresh produce and local wine, an afternoon siesta in the shade of a vine-covered pergola, fresh coffee in a sun-drenched courtyard—the Italians have been enjoying the outdoor room philosophy for years.

Italy is romantic and unhurried, yet vibrant and passionate at the same time. Here, there is no distinction between indoor and outdoor living; the term 'alfresco', which literally translates as 'in the open air', has long been a part of Italian culture. Most importantly, it is instilled in every Italian that anything normally done inside—from relaxing and sleeping to eating and entertaining and even working—can also be done outside.

Italy occupies a long, boot-shaped peninsula in southern Europe and includes Sardinia, Sicily and several smaller islands. To the north, the Alps form a natural boundary with France, Switzerland, Austria and Slovenia and elsewhere the country is surrounded by sea. The climate varies considerably. In the south, the coastal areas are typically Mediterranean with mild winters and warm, generally dry summers; in the interior weather can vary due to the higher altitudes and valleys and, particularly during winter months, it tends to be cold, wet and often snowy. Inland to the north, there is a more humid and subtropical 'continental' climate.

Italians have long been recognised for their affinity with the land. In Ancient Rome, country 'pleasure' gardens provided a refuge from urban life—a place of peace and tranquillity where emperors and dignitaries could entertain and seek respite from their stately duties. The Roman reverence for running water ensured there were always many water features throughout these gardens. Grapevines or frescos decorated the courtyard walls and the landscaping was designed to enhance and maximise the sweeping views, while local orchards and vegetable gardens provided the bounty for magnificent feasts.

During the Italian Renaissance, the ruling power of the aristocracy was reflected in elaborate garden design on a massive scale. Intended to impress and demonstrate control, these extraordinary gardens were formal and geometric in their planting, with orderly arrangements, neatly trimmed box hedges, ornate sculptures depicting scenes from ancient mythology and giant water features and fountains symbolising fertility and abundance.

But perhaps the biggest historical influence in garden style arose from the two world wars, during which many Italians were forced to rely almost entirely on food cultivated in their own plots. Limitations on transport and agriculture caused by the wars required the average family garden to be functional as well as aesthetic, providing vegetables and fruit for the owners.

Today, the need for both formal and functional areas remains an essential part of Italian garden design. Ingrained from generations past, modern Italians still aspire to their own kitchen garden or *l'orto*—usually as close to the house as possible—for easy access to fresh, organic vegetables and herbs. Also essential is an outdoor entertaining area, or simple terrace of stone or terracotta tiles, decorated with pots of trees with flowers spilling over the rims, urns and vases—the more rustic the better. Some sort of overhead pergola may also be in place, in traditional wood or more contemporary metal, but always large enough to shelter a table and chairs for leisurely dining. Finally, a *loggia* or similar shaded structure, in which eating, sleeping and reading can all be done in shady seclusion, may be attached to or separate from the house. Alfresco living and dining at its best! No wonder I feel at home here.

inspired design ideas

WATER FEATURE WITH FRESCO BACKDROP

Water features and fresco paintings are typical of Italian garden design. The Italian reverence for running water—symbolic of fertility and abundance—is reflected in large, impressive water features. Vibrant and colourful frescoes of farm life and Italian scenery adorn many of the walls of small courtyard gardens.

SPILL-OVER PLANTS

In Roman times, pots filled with flowers spilling over the sides added colour to courtyards without taxing the water supply. Vine-covered arbours, pergolas and even houses offer shade, and window boxes filled with cascading plants such as bougainvillea (*Bougainvillea*), ivy geranium (*Pelargonium*) and Chilean jasmine (*Mandevilla*) soften the walls of buildings.

POTTERY AND CERAMICS

One of the main features in Italian garden design is the use of vases, urns and pots to grow plants or as *objets d'art*. Often worked-in or cracked, they add a rustic charm to any garden or courtyard. Courtyards lined with citrus topiaries standing in large terracotta pots are as commonplace today as they were hundreds of years ago.

PARTERRES

During the Renaissance, garden design was on such a grand scale that gardens could almost be considered outdoor extensions of palace rooms. Orderly and formal, the geometric lines were defined by neatly trimmed box hedges (*Buxus*) and mazes, separating different areas of the garden and marking the beginning of the parterre garden.

PIZZA OVEN

Round ovens built from brick and local stone have long been a part of Italian heritage. Often owned by individual families, they originated in Naples and were very rustic, with a base made from wood and sticks and a layer of rough terracotta bricks stacked in a criss-cross fashion on top. These rustic ovens formed the foundation of Italy's modern pizza oven industry.

italy at home

Family is the most important thing to the owners of this suburban home and, with a large extended family, there are always plenty of get-togethers and celebrations. It's not surprising, then, that top of their garden wish list was an entertaining area. This family needed a defined space for entertaining and gathering, but also a kitchen garden for their home-grown vegetables and herbs.

The house had a small balcony at the rear with steps down to a level lawn. We attached terracotta planter pots to the railings of the balcony and planted brightly coloured Chilean jasmine (*Mandevilla*) and ivy geranium (*Pelargonium*) to spill over and cascade down in Roman style.

In keeping with Italian garden style and the owners' requirements, we wanted to ensure the living areas were balanced with a functional kitchen garden. Using timber sleepers we built a new vegetable garden in place of the original, raising it to waist height to make it more accessible for the elderly couple. After lining the interior of the garden to prevent the timber treatment leaching into the soil we planted a mix of culinary herbs. We built an outdoor wood-fired pizza oven and created an entertaining area where the whole family could gather and share meals. The table was made from a pre-cut slab of marble and as an interesting feature—inspired from a 500-year-old table I saw at Villa Lante in Italy—we cut out a hole in the centre and inserted several stainless steel troughs to be used as storage for chilled wine or herbs.

Next, I designed a stylised feature area with a modern parterre cut into the paving—a pattern made of cream-coloured concrete pavers with synthetic turf between them. This was marked on each corner by a double box hedge (*Buxus*

Microphylla var. japonica) clipped to different heights, with topiaried sparten juniper (*Juniperus chinensis* 'Spartan') planted in large earthenware pots. Triple-stepped box hedges link all the corners. The overall effect is a window into the grandeur and symmetry of a typical Italian Renaissance garden.

Beyond this paving, an ordinary pool fence was replaced with clear, frameless glass to give the illusion of depth. Pebblecrete coping was replaced with Bullnose terracotta pavers in keeping with the Italian style. We then built an arbour consisting of timber beams, to which we added terracotta troughs and masses of spill-over Chilean jasmine (*Mandevilla*). At the entry to the pool area and on either side of the arbour we placed two advanced olive trees (*Olea europaea* var. communis) in pots. Three citrus tress (*Citrus* x *aurantiifolia* 'Tahiti') in terracotta urns were placed around the garden.

On the far wall at the back of the property we attached a fresco painting of the Trevi Fountain done on flexible fibre mesh sourced and custom-painted by an Italian artist. A concrete clam shell from an existing water feature was incorporated into the design, helping to make the entertaining area not just about the immediate garden but also the view—by drawing the eye across the lawn and parterre paving, through the arbour and across the pool to the magnificent artwork and relaxation area. We dressed up the walls of this space by adding three pairs of timber shutters and decorative plates brought back from my trip to Italy. Combined with rustic troughs with more spill-over planting and comfortable outdoor furniture, these simple additions turn this space into something resembling the outside of a Italian villa.

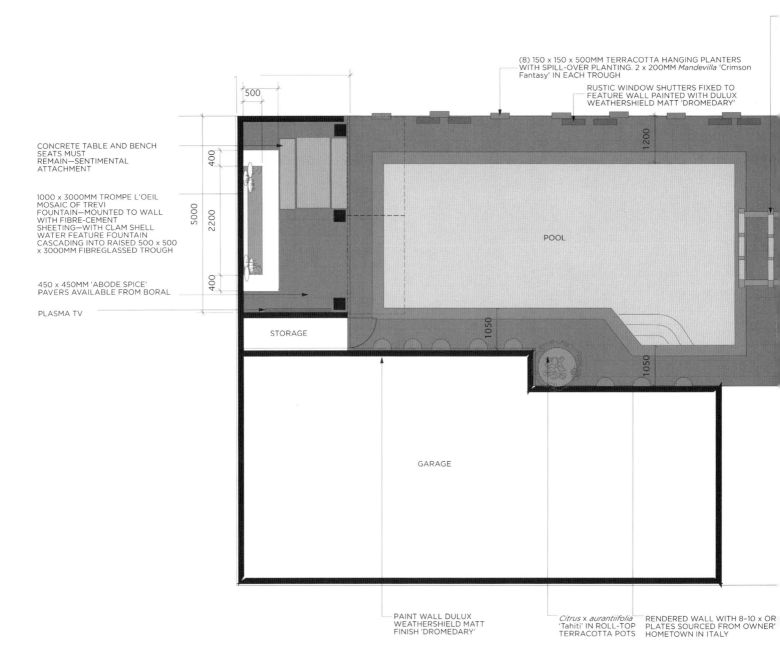

(8) 150 x 150 x 500MM TERRACOTTA HANGING PLANTERS
WITH SPILL-OVER PLANTING. 2 x 200MM *Mandevilla* 'Crimson
Fantasy' IN EACH TROUGH

RUSTIC WINDOW SHUTTERS FIXED TO
FEATURE WALL PAINTED WITH DULUX
WEATHERSHIELD MATT 'DROMEDARY'

CONCRETE TABLE AND BENCH
SEATS MUST
REMAIN—SENTIMENTAL
ATTACHMENT

1000 x 3000MM TROMPE L'OEIL
MOSAIC OF TREVI
FOUNTAIN—MOUNTED TO WALL
WITH FIBRE-CEMENT
SHEETING—WITH CLAM SHELL
WATER FEATURE FOUNTAIN
CASCADING INTO RAISED 500 x 500
x 3000MM FIBREGLASSED TROUGH

450 x 450MM 'ABODE SPICE'
PAVERS AVAILABLE FROM BORAL

PLASMA TV

POOL

STORAGE

GARAGE

500

400

5000

2200

400

1200

1050

1050

PAINT WALL DULUX
WEATHERSHIELD MATT
FINISH 'DROMEDARY'

Citrus x *aurantiifolia*
'Tahiti' IN ROLL-TOP
TERRACOTTA POTS

RENDERED WALL WITH 8-10 x OR
PLATES SOURCED FROM OWNER'
HOMETOWN IN ITALY

Note: Plans may vary from design to construction

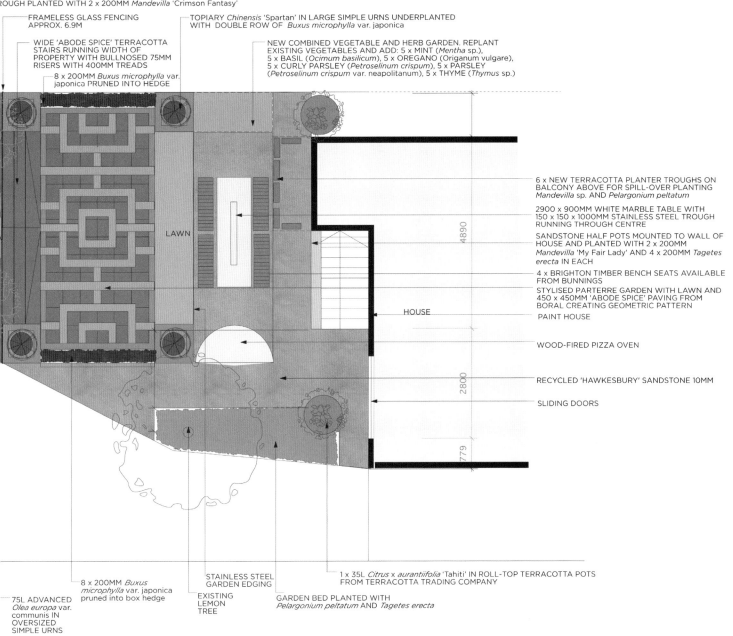

ARBOUR WITH PLANTER TROUGHS FOR SPILL-OVER PLANTING.
ROUGH PLANTED WITH 2 x 200MM *Mandevilla* 'Crimson Fantasy'

FRAMELESS GLASS FENCING
APPROX. 6.9M

TOPIARY *Chinensis* 'Spartan' IN LARGE SIMPLE URNS UNDERPLANTED
WITH DOUBLE ROW OF *Buxus microphylla* var. japonica

WIDE 'ABODE SPICE' TERRACOTTA
STAIRS RUNNING WIDTH OF
PROPERTY WITH BULLNOSED 75MM
RISERS WITH 400MM TREADS

NEW COMBINED VEGETABLE AND HERB GARDEN. REPLANT
EXISTING VEGETABLES AND ADD: 5 x MINT (*Mentha* sp.),
5 x BASIL (*Ocimum basilicum*), 5 x OREGANO (Origanum vulgare),
5 x CURLY PARSLEY (*Petroselinum crispum*), 5 x PARSLEY
(*Petroselinum crispum* var. neapolitanum), 5 x THYME (*Thymus* sp.)

8 x 200MM *Buxus microphylla* var.
japonica PRUNED INTO HEDGE

LAWN

6 x NEW TERRACOTTA PLANTER TROUGHS ON
BALCONY ABOVE FOR SPILL-OVER PLANTING
Mandevilla sp. AND *Pelargonium peltatum*

2900 x 900MM WHITE MARBLE TABLE WITH
150 x 150 x 1000MM STAINLESS STEEL TROUGH
RUNNING THROUGH CENTRE

SANDSTONE HALF POTS MOUNTED TO WALL OF
HOUSE AND PLANTED WITH 2 x 200MM
Mandevilla 'My Fair Lady' AND 4 x 200MM *Tagetes
erecta* IN EACH

4 x BRIGHTON TIMBER BENCH SEATS AVAILABLE
FROM BUNNINGS

STYLISED PARTERRE GARDEN WITH LAWN AND
450 x 450MM 'ABODE SPICE' PAVING FROM
BORAL CREATING GEOMETRIC PATTERN

PAINT HOUSE

HOUSE

4890

2800

779

WOOD-FIRED PIZZA OVEN

RECYCLED 'HAWKESBURY' SANDSTONE 10MM

SLIDING DOORS

8 x 200MM *Buxus
microphylla* var. japonica
pruned into box hedge

STAINLESS STEEL
GARDEN EDGING

EXISTING
LEMON
TREE

1 x 35L *Citrus x aurantiifolia* 'Tahiti' IN ROLL-TOP TERRACOTTA POTS
FROM TERRACOTTA TRADING COMPANY

75L ADVANCED
Olea europa var.
communis IN
OVERSIZED
SIMPLE URNS

GARDEN BED PLANTED WITH
Pelargonium peltatum AND *Tagetes erecta*

This page—clockwise from bottom left:

• The boundary wall was transformed by painting it Tuscan burnt orange and adding weathered shutters in a contrasting pale green. Flowers in terracotta planters add a cosy villa-style feel.

• Around the pool, Italian-style terracotta pavers replace the original pebblecrete and a new frameless glass fence opens up the space creating the illusion of depth. Defined by a timber arbour with masses of cascading plants, the view is now uninterrupted from the entertaining area to the parterre paving, pool and artwork beyond.

• The parterre-style paving is one of the main features of this garden. Framed by box hedge (*Buxus microphylla* var. japonica) and topiaried spartan juniper (*Chinensis* 'Spartan') in large earthenware pots, the symmetry of this area is reminiscent of Italian Renaissance style.

Facing page—from top:

• The table, made from a slab of pre-cut white marble on top of rendered blocks, features several stainless steel troughs perfect for holding chilled wine and herbs, and is large enough for plenty of family and friends to gather around.

• We introduced a variety of different-sized pots and planters with masses of bright spill-over flowers, and citrus and olive trees to add Italian-style character and charm. They soften the area and enhance the courtyard atmosphere.

design key

Create your own Italian-style outdoor living space by incorporating some of the ideas we came up with for our garden. Allowing space for a kitchen garden can be a practical and enjoyable investment—consider aspects such as ease of access and proximity to the home and water sources.

PLANTS

TREES
- *Citrus x aurantiifolia* 'Tahiti' TAHITIAN LIME (4)
- *Chinensis* 'Spartan' SPARTAN JUNIPER
- *Olea europa* var. communis OLIVE

SHRUBS
- *Buxus microphylla* var. japonica JAPANESE BOX
- *Mandevilla* 'My Fair Lady' CHILEAN JASMINE (3)
- *Mandevilla* 'Red Riding Hood' CHILEAN JASMINE (2)
- *Mandevilla* 'Crimson Fantasy' CHILEAN JASMINE
- *Pelargonium peltatum* IVY GERANIUM

HERBS, VEGETABLES AND FLOWERS
- *Cosmos bipinnatus* COSMOS (1)
- *Mentha sp.* MINT
- *Ocimum basilicum* BASIL
- *Origanum vulgare* OREGANO
- *Petroselinum crispum* CURLY PARSLEY
- *Petroselinum crispum* var. neapolitanum PARSLEY
- *Tagetes erecta* MARIGOLD
- *Thymus sp.* THYME

MATERIALS

WALLS
- Fabric drapes and an artwork screen the wall of the shed at the rear of the garden (5).
- The boundary walls and fences were painted with Tuscan burnt-orange tones (3).
- Recycled timber shutter doors were unhinged, separated, cut in half and painted in a pale green distressed finish before being attached to the boundary walls (3).

FLOORS
- Terracotta pavers replace pebblecrete around the pool and in the entertaining area.
- Cream-coloured concrete pavers and synthetic turf make the parterre. Light-coloured paving was used here to distinguish this feature from the rest of the garden (4).

OVERHEAD
- Timber-framed arbour made from treated pine and painted with whitewash (2).

FEATURES
- A large fresco artwork painted on flexible fibre mesh by an Italian painter and mounted in a plaster frame is attached to the rear wall. A concrete clam shell recycled from an existing water feature forms part of the feature (1, 5).
- An outdoor pizza oven assembled on site and built in forms an integral part of the entertaining area.

FURNITURE
AND ACCESSORIES

1 Traditional decorative plates sourced from Italy add character and charm to the Tuscan walls.

2 Stainless steel troughs embedded into the table are both decorative and practical. Ideal for storing chilled wine, fresh flowers or planted-in herbs.

3 Comfortable outdoor armchairs, day bed and chaise lounge are arranged around the pool and relaxation area. Made of synthetic wicker they are hard-wearing and can withstand all weather conditions, making them ideal for outdoor use.

4 A quaint country-style jug with hand-painted rooster design and matching salt and pepper shakers add to the provincial look and feel of the garden.

5 This terracotta cherub, also sourced from Italy, adds a decorative element to the arbour.

6 The dining setting, cutlery and napkins tie in with the rustic pottery look and overall colour palette. A glazed pottery decanter and cup set brought back from Italy complements the setting.

7 Italian tapestries and brocade fabrics in burnt-orange cotton and sea-green damask add comfort and complement the painted surfaces.

JAMIE BROUGHT HOME:

■ Pottery from owner's hometown in Italy

■ Terracotta trinkets to add to owner's own collection

Look out for similar Italian and Italian-inspired items at markets and stores in your area.

acknowledgements

Putting a book together like this one with gardens, ideas and great information takes a big group effort and I must start by thanking the team at HarperCollins Publishers for their never-ending belief and constant support. To everyone at Channel 7 for finally giving me the chance to turn *The Outdoor Room* into a reality after 4 years of pitches; the Landart boys for the late nights, the grunts, sweat and all my last-minute changes; the PATIO Landscape Architecture and Design and JPD MEDIA family for all of manner of random requests and attention to detail and to all at JD PUBLISHING for putting up with my schedule, working to incredibly tight deadlines and for making this project happen—as always I could not have done this without you all and I've enjoyed every moment of creating this book ... thank you.

I would also like to acknowledge the invaluable support of our suppliers:

Allplastics Engineering • 02 9417 6111 • www.allplastics.com.au
Amber Tiles • 1300 362 241 • www.ambertiles.com.au
ASG Safety Glass • 1300 30 30 60 • www.asgsafetyglass.com.au
Austimber Supplies Pty Ltd • 02 9627 5001 • www.austimbersupplies.com.au
Australian Native Landscapes • 131 458 • www.anlscape.com.au
BeefEater Barbeques • 1800 356 660 • www.beefeaterbbq.com
Better Bricks and Paving • 03 5249 4555 • www.betterbricks.com.au
Boral • 1300 134 002 • www.boral.com.au/landscaping
Boral Roof Tiles • 1300 363 072 • www.boral.com.au/outdoorroom
Bosch • 1300 368 339 • www.boschappliances.com.au
Chippy's Outdoor • 03 9879 4296 • www.chippystimber.com.au
Contour Ponds and Pumps • 02 9690 2688 • www.pondliners.com.au
CSR Cemintel • 1300 CEMINTEL/1300 2364 6835 • www.cemintel.com.au
CSR Gyprock • 1300 306 556 • www.gyprock.com.au
CSR Hebel • 1300 369 448 • www.hebelaustralia.com.au
DATS Skip Bins • 1300 654 334 • www.datsskipbins.com.au
Dawa Stone Australia Pty Ltd • 02 9799 8377 • www.dawastone.com.au
Direct Pickets • 03 9335 1048 • www.directpickets.com.au
Disegno Carbone • 02 9743 4999 • www.disegnocarbone.com.au
Dulux • 132 525 • www.dulux.com.au
Electrolux Integrated Barbecue • 1300 363 640 • www.electrolux.com.au
Everdure • 1300 766 066 • www.everdure.com
Finlayson's Timber and Hardware Pty Ltd • 07 3393 0588 • www.finlayson.com.au
The Fire Company • 02 9997 3050 • www.thefirecompany.com.au
HG Turf Pty Ltd • 1800 622 340 • www.hgturf.com.au
House of Bamboo • 02 9666 5703 • www.houseofbamboo.com.au
Imperial Gardens • 02 9450 2455 • www.imperialgardens.com.au
Interior Art Image • 02 9380 2242 • www.interiorartimage.com
Japanache • 02 4871 1388 • www.japanache.com.au
Keverton Outdoor Pty Ltd • 03 9889 6542 • www.kevertonoutdoor.com.au
Leaf & Stone Garden Gallery • 03 5221 8083 • www.leafandstone.com.au
Marblo Glazia Pty Ltd • 02 9683 7788 • www.marblo.com.au
Mediterranean Woodfired Ovens • 1300 883 909 • www.woodfiredovens.com.au
Melton Craft • 03 9360 0150 • www.meltoncraft.com.au
Monsoon Trading • 041 241 3479 • www.monsoontrading.com.au
National Hire • 136 336 • www.nationalhire.com.au
Origin Energy • 132 461 • www.originenergy.com.au
Ozsun Shade Systems • 02 9557 2251 • www.ozsun.com.au
Panasonic • 132 600 • www.panasonic.com.au
PGH Bricks & Pavers • 131 579 • www.pghbricks.com.au
Potsonline • 02 9651 3971 • www.potsonline.com.au
Rock 'n' Stone • 03 9571 6266 • www.rocknstone.com.au
Samsara Furniture & Homewares Pty Ltd • 07 5538 0177 • www.samsarafurniture.com.au
SsangYong • www.ssangyong.com.au
Sunbeam • 1300 881 861 • www.sunbeam.com.au
Sydney Pots Factory • 02 9687 4688
Tic Tac Tours and Charters • 1300 887 837 • www.tictactours.com.au
Tropical Thatch Pty Ltd • 1300 781 104 • www.tropicalthatch.com.au
Veolia Environmental Services • 1300 13 53 53 • www.veolia.com.au
Warwick Fabrics (Australia) Pty Ltd • 03 9419 7544 • www.warwick.com.au
Yarrabee & Castlemaine Stone Solutions • 03 9535 1500 • www.yarrabee.com.au